TROLL BRIDGE™

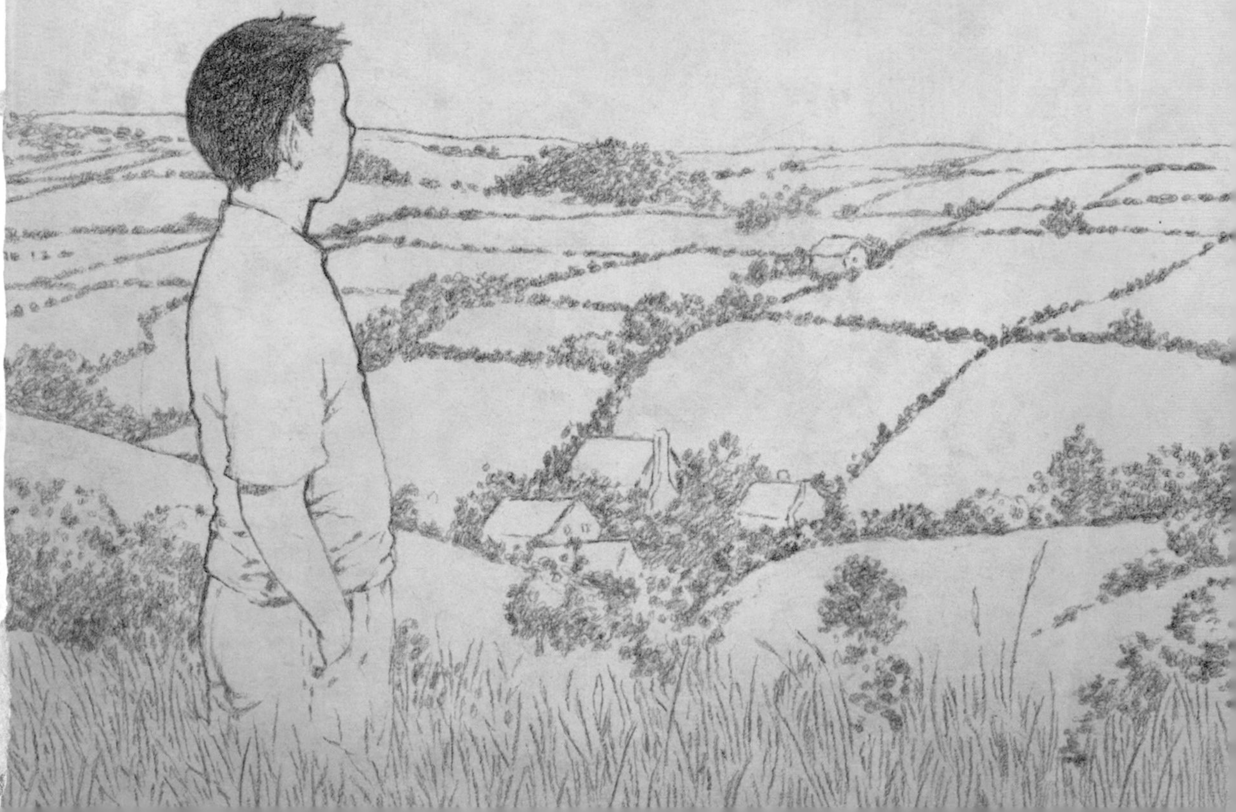

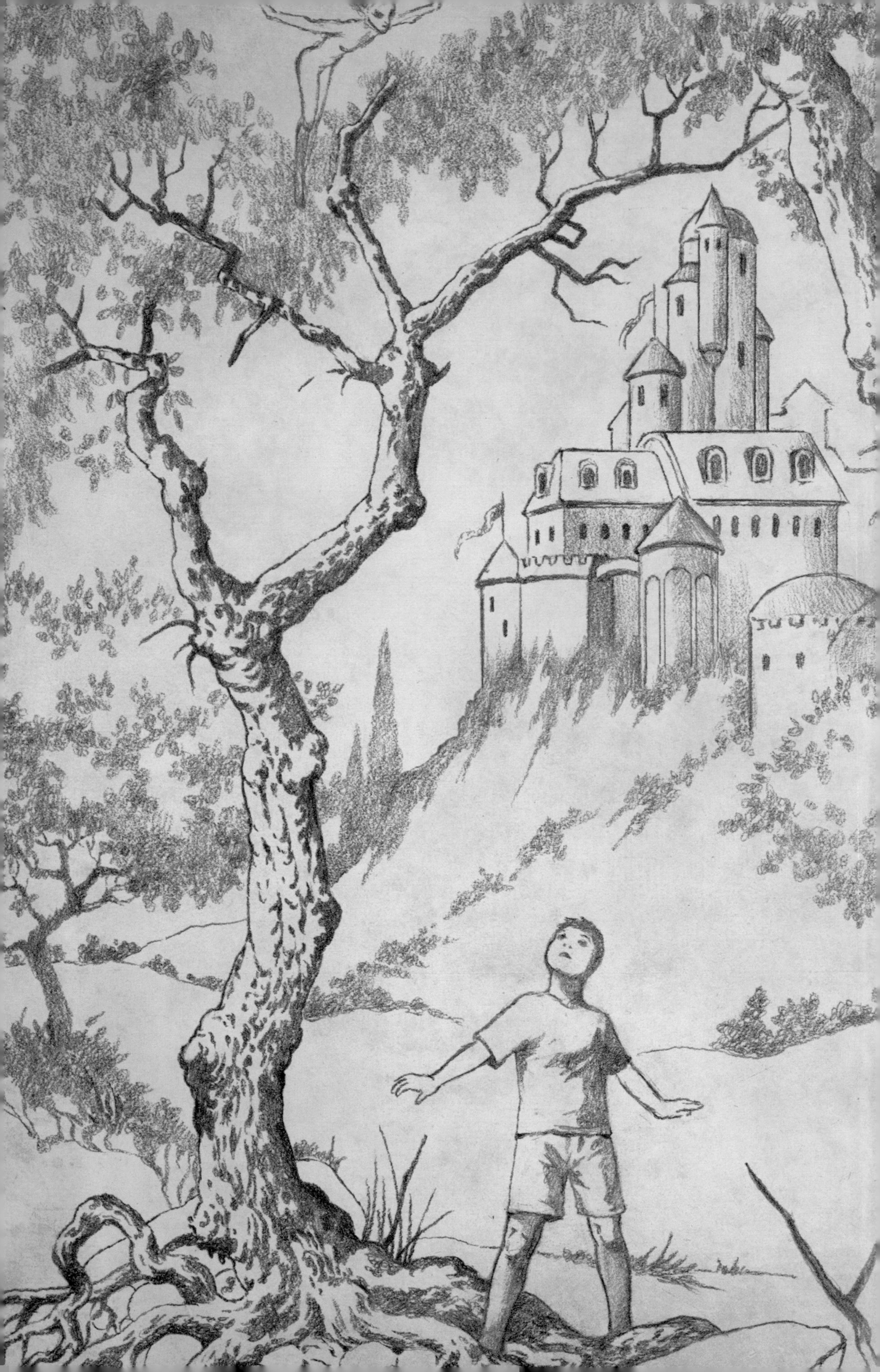

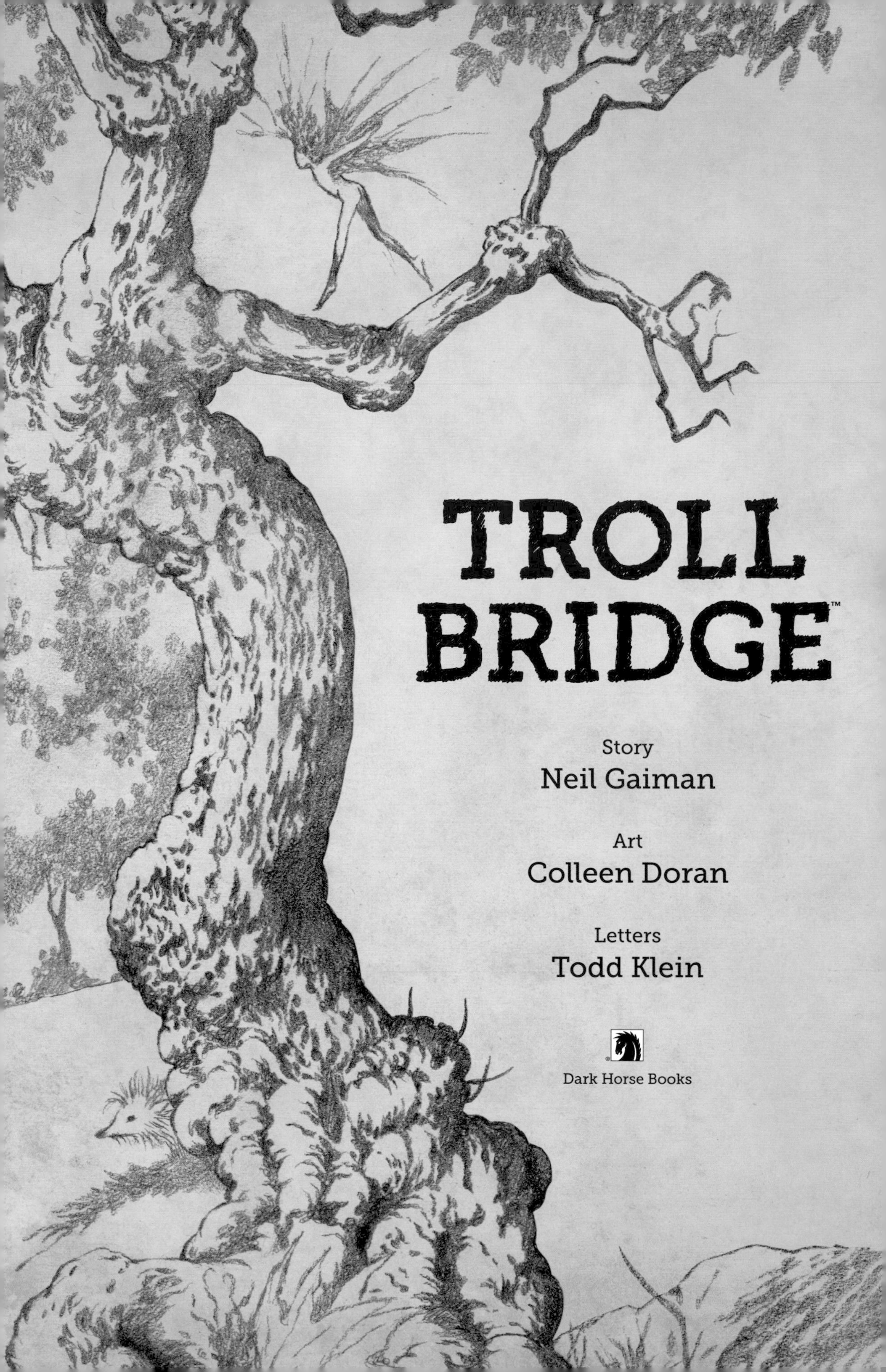

TROLL BRIDGE™

Story
Neil Gaiman

Art
Colleen Doran

Letters
Todd Klein

Dark Horse Books

President and Publisher
MIKE RICHARDSON

Editors
DIANA SCHUTZ and DANIEL CHABON

Assistant Editor
CARDNER CLARK

Designer
ETHAN KIMBERLING

Digital Art Technician
ALLYSON HALLER

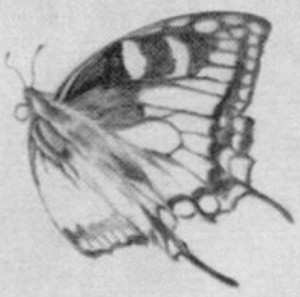

Neil Hankerson, Executive Vice President | Tom Weddle, Chief Financial Officer | Randy Stradley, Vice President of Publishing | Michael Martens, Vice President of Book Trade Sales | Matt Parkinson, Vice President of Marketing | David Scroggy, Vice President of Product Development | Dale LaFountain, Vice President of Information Technology | Cara Niece, Vice President of Production and Scheduling | Nick McWhorter, Vice President of Media Licensing | Ken Lizzi, General Counsel | Dave Marshall, Editor in Chief | Davey Estrada, Editorial Director | Scott Allie, Executive Senior Editor | Chris Warner, Senior Books Editor | Cary Grazzini, Director of Print and Development | Lia Ribacchi, Art Director | Mark Bernardi, Director of Digital Publishing | Michael Gombos, Director of International Publishing and Licensing

Published by Dark Horse Books
A division of Dark Horse Comics, Inc.
10956 SE Main Street
Milwaukie, OR 97222

First edition: September 2016
ISBN 978-1-50670-008-3

1 3 5 7 9 10 8 6 4 2
Printed in China

International Licensing: (503) 905-2377
Comic Shop Locator Service: (888) 266-4226

Neil Gaiman's Troll Bridge

Library of Congress Cataloging-in-Publication Data

Names: Gaiman, Neil, author. | Doran, Colleen, illustrator. | Klein, Todd, illustrator.
Title: Troll bridge / story, Neil Gaiman ; art, Colleen Doran ; letters, Todd Klein.
Description: First edition. | Milwaukie, OR : Dark Horse Books, 2016.
Identifiers: LCCN 2016014645 | ISBN 9781506700083 (hardback)
Subjects: LCSH: Graphic novels. | BISAC: COMICS & GRAPHIC NOVELS / Fantasy.
Classification: LCC PN6737.G3 T76 2016 | DDC 741.5/942--dc23
LC record available at https://lccn.loc.gov/2016014645

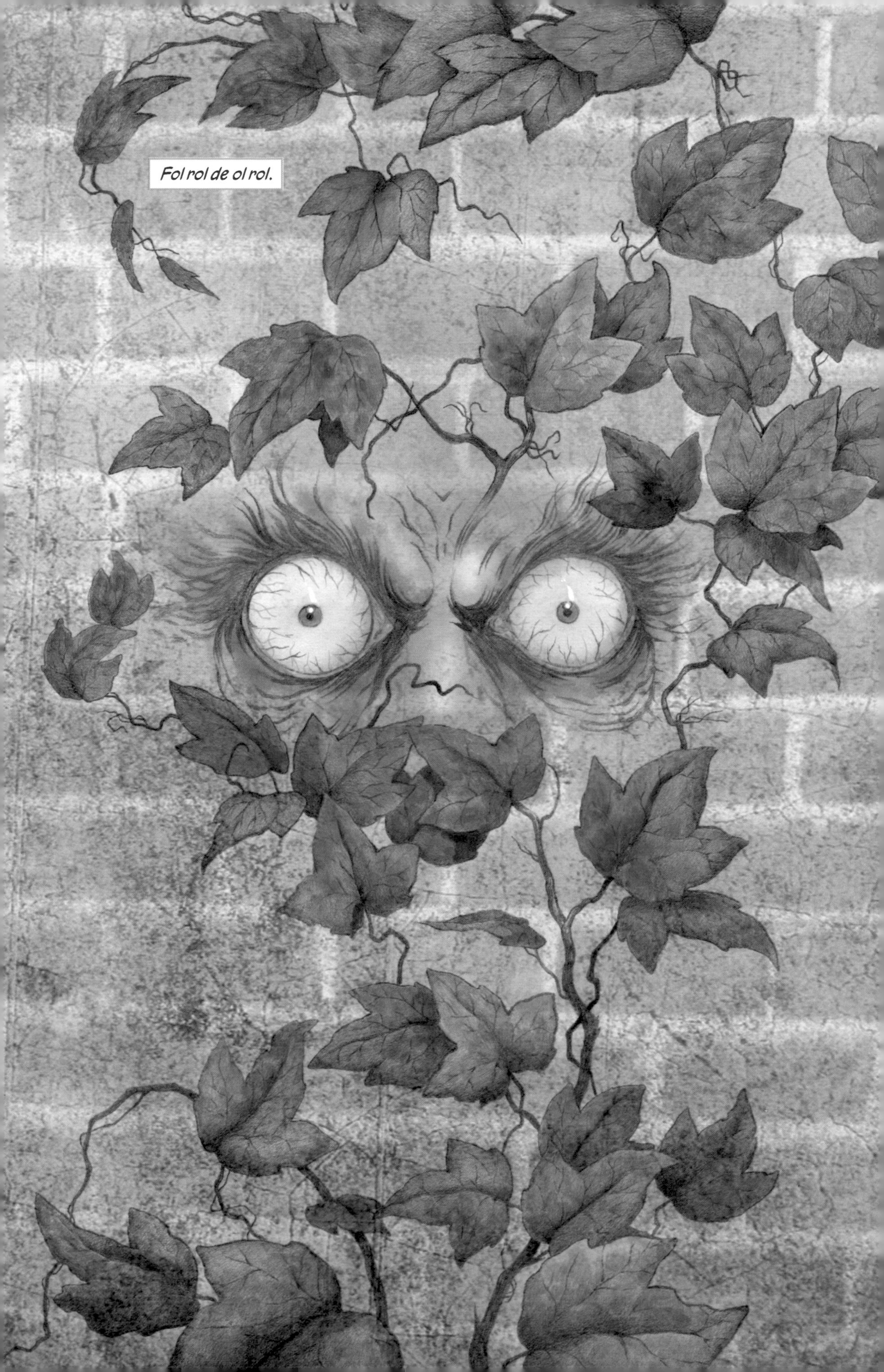
Fol rol de ol rol.

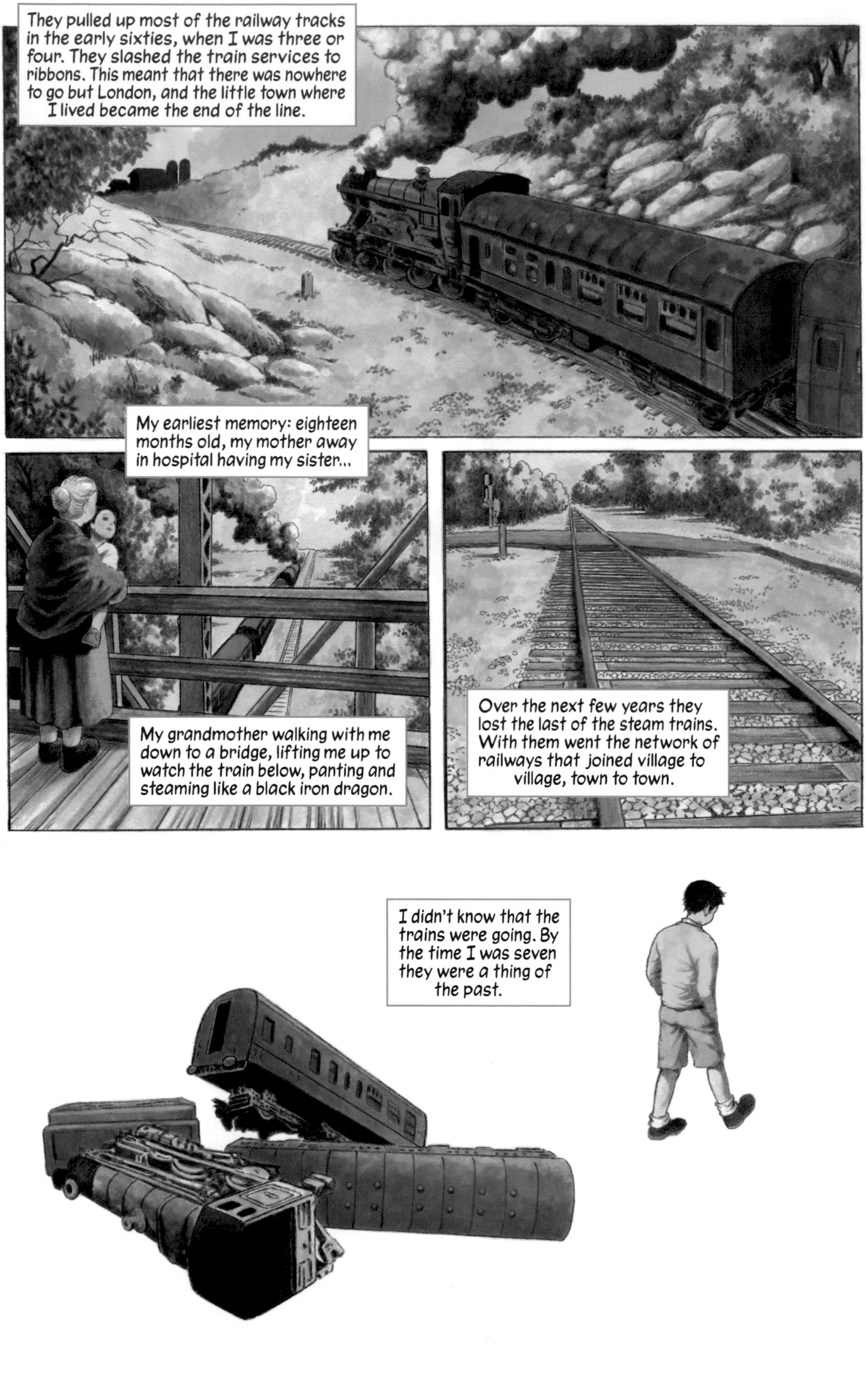
They pulled up most of the railway tracks in the early sixties, when I was three or four. They slashed the train services to ribbons. This meant that there was nowhere to go but London, and the little town where I lived became the end of the line.
My earliest memory: eighteen months old, my mother away in hospital having my sister...
My grandmother walking with me down to a bridge, lifting me up to watch the train below, panting and steaming like a black iron dragon.
Over the next few years they lost the last of the steam trains. With them went the network of railways that joined village to village, town to town.
I didn't know that the trains were going. By the time I was seven they were a thing of the past.

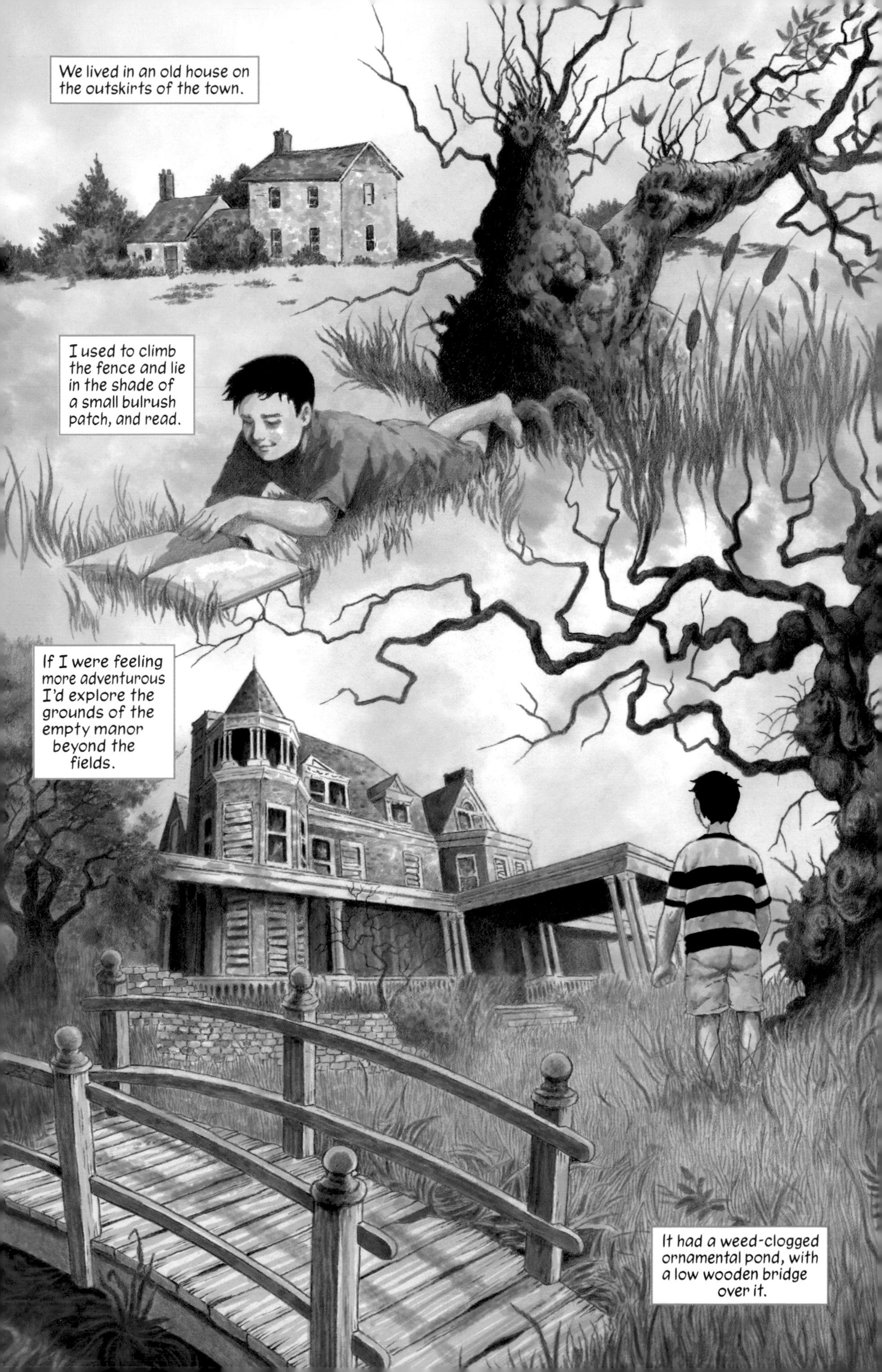
We lived in an old house on the outskirts of the town.
I used to climb the fence and lie in the shade of a small bulrush patch, and read.
If I were feeling more adventurous I'd explore the grounds of the empty manor beyond the fields.
It had a weed-clogged ornamental pond, with a low wooden bridge over it.

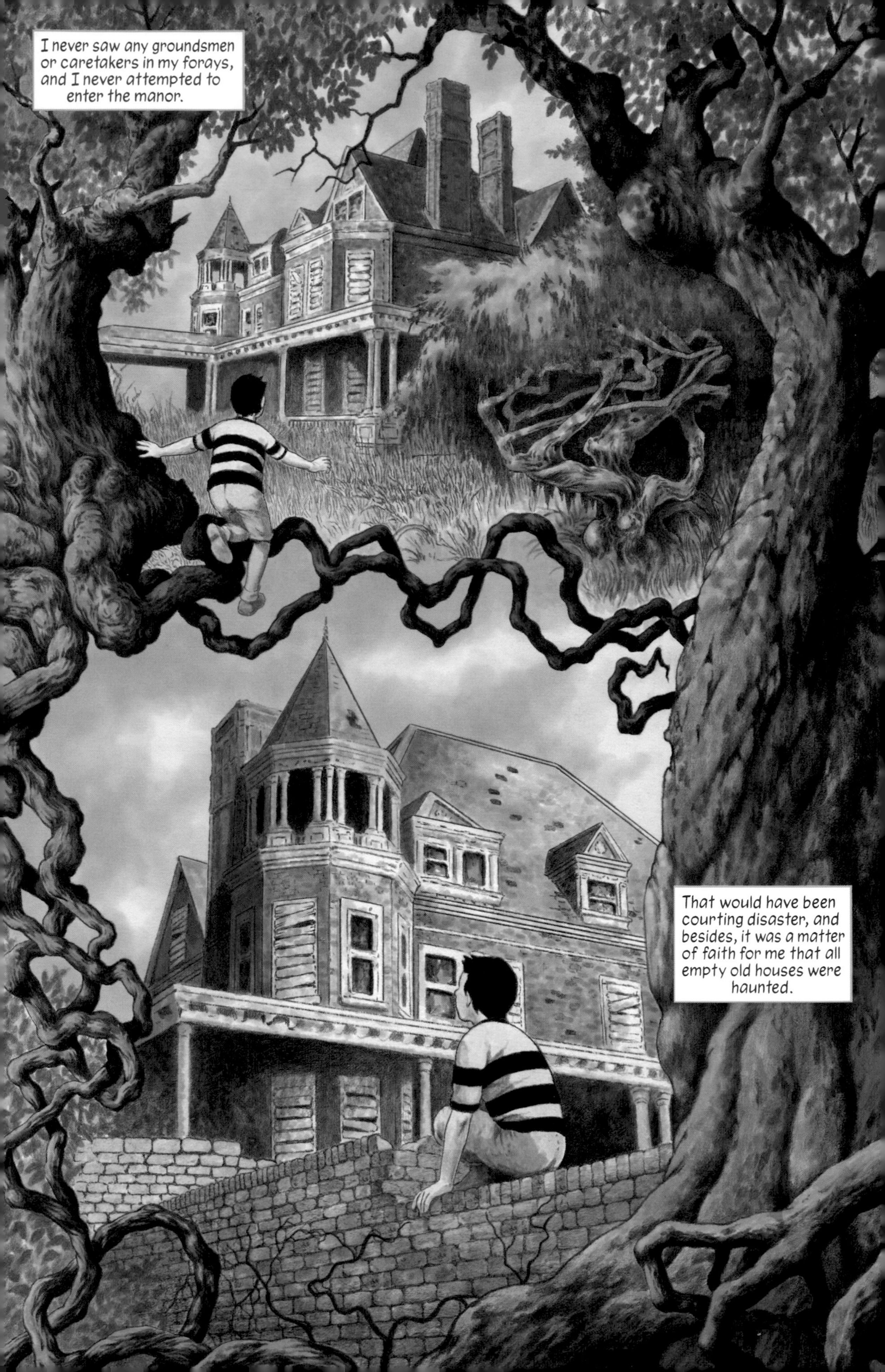
I never saw any groundsmen or caretakers in my forays, and I never attempted to enter the manor.
That would have been courting disaster, and besides, it was a matter of faith for me that all empty old houses were haunted.

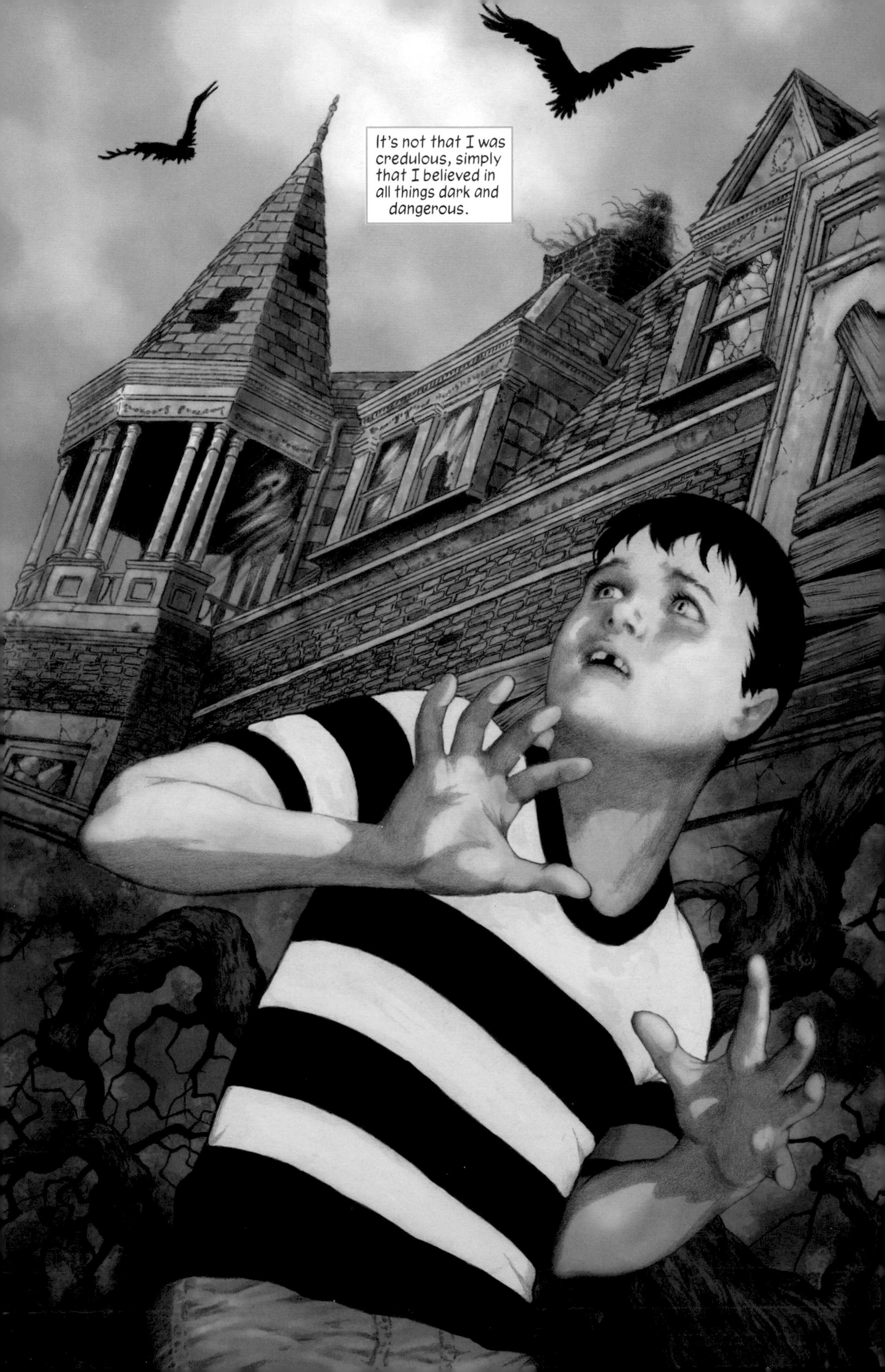
It's not that I was credulous, simply that I believed in all things dark and dangerous.

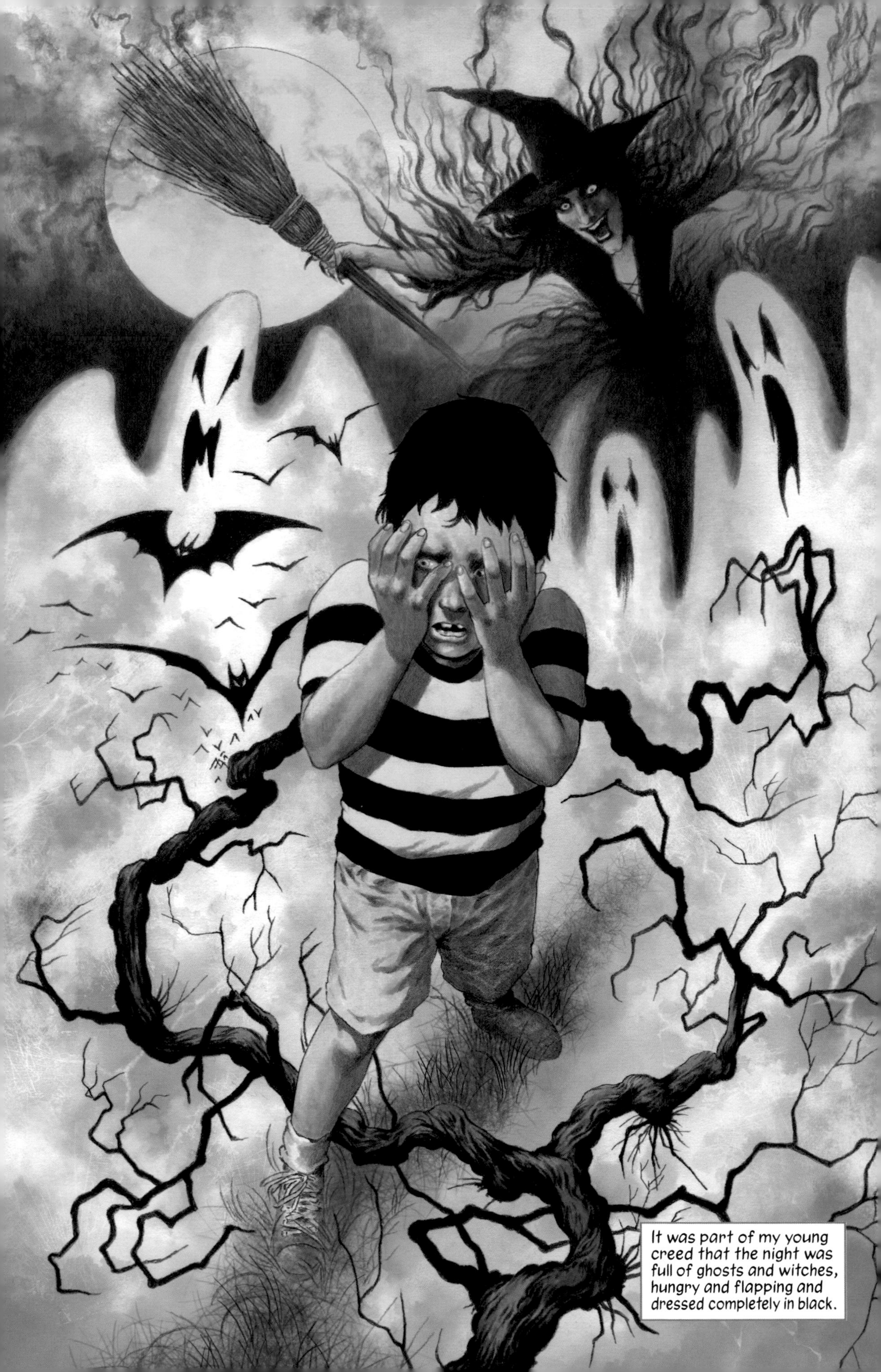
It was part of my young creed that the night was full of ghosts and witches, hungry and flapping and dressed completely in black.

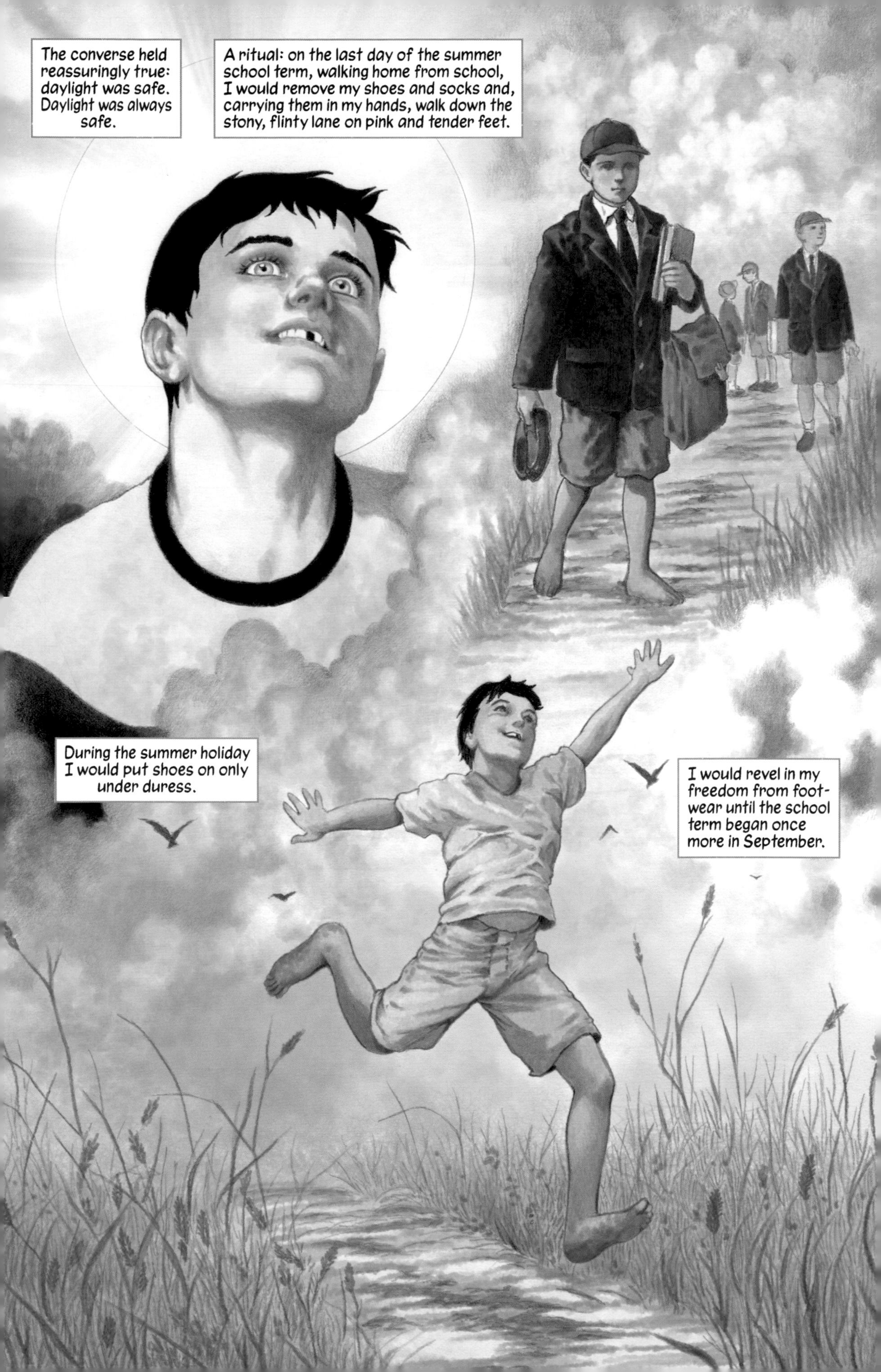
The converse held reassuringly true: daylight was safe. Daylight was always safe.
A ritual: on the last day of the summer school term, walking home from school, I would remove my shoes and socks and, carrying them in my hands, walk down the stony, flinty lane on pink and tender feet.
During the summer holiday I would put shoes on only under duress.
I would revel in my freedom from foot-wear until the school term began once more in September.

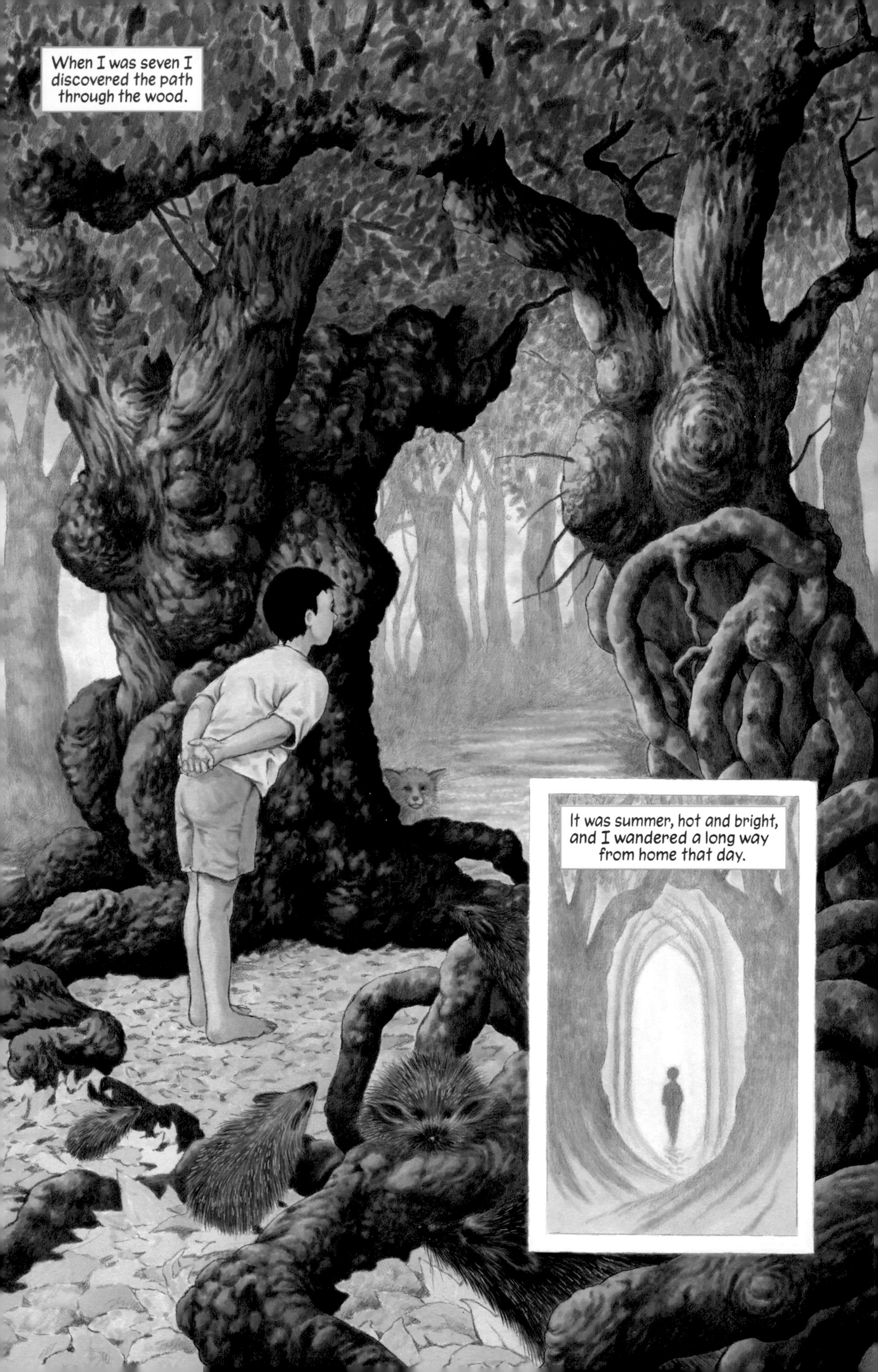
When I was seven I discovered the path through the wood.
It was summer, hot and bright, and I wandered a long way from home that day.

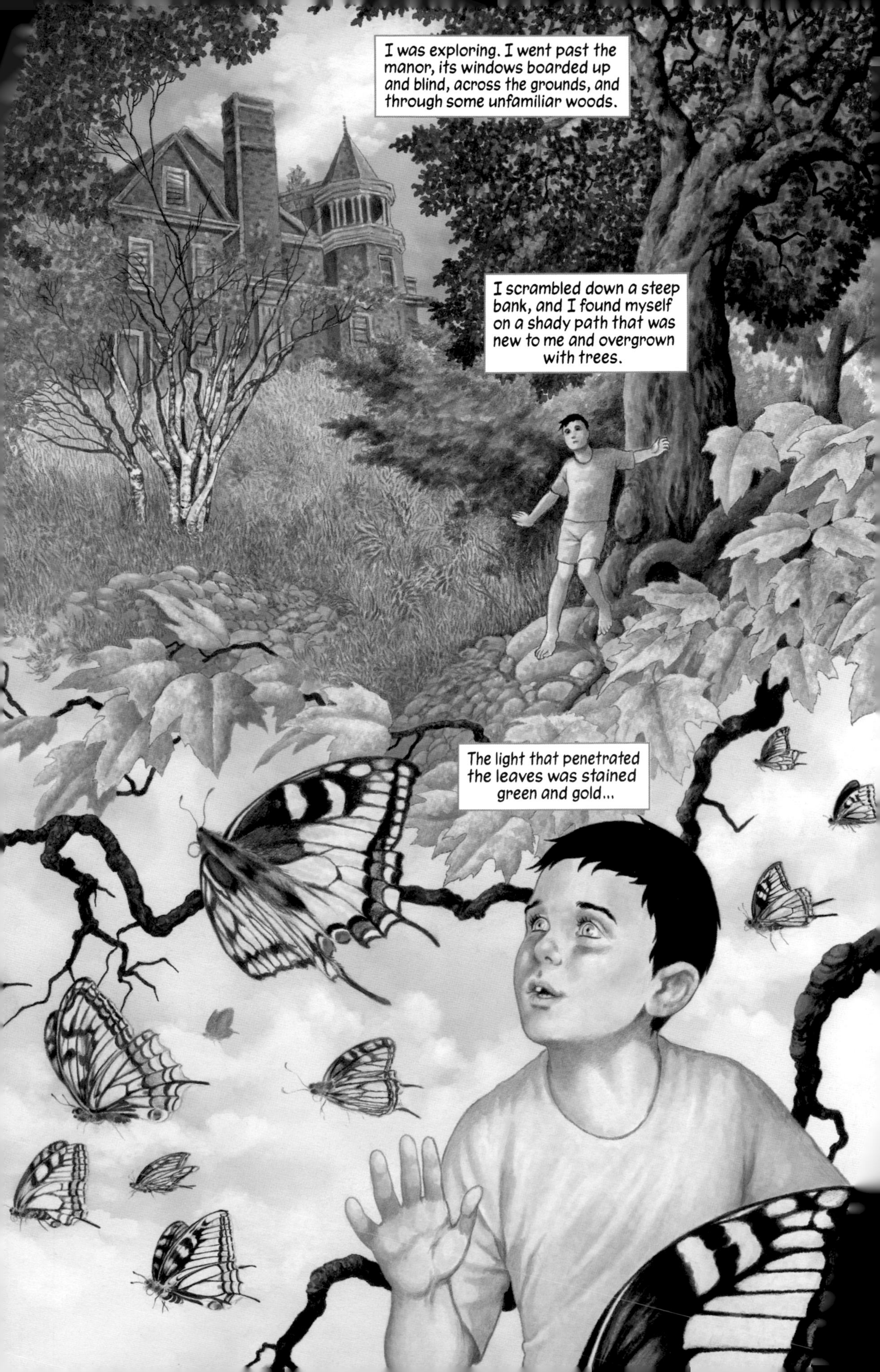
I was exploring. I went past the manor, its windows boarded up and blind, across the grounds, and through some unfamiliar woods.
I scrambled down a steep bank, and I found myself on a shady path that was new to me and overgrown with trees.
The light that penetrated the leaves was stained green and gold...

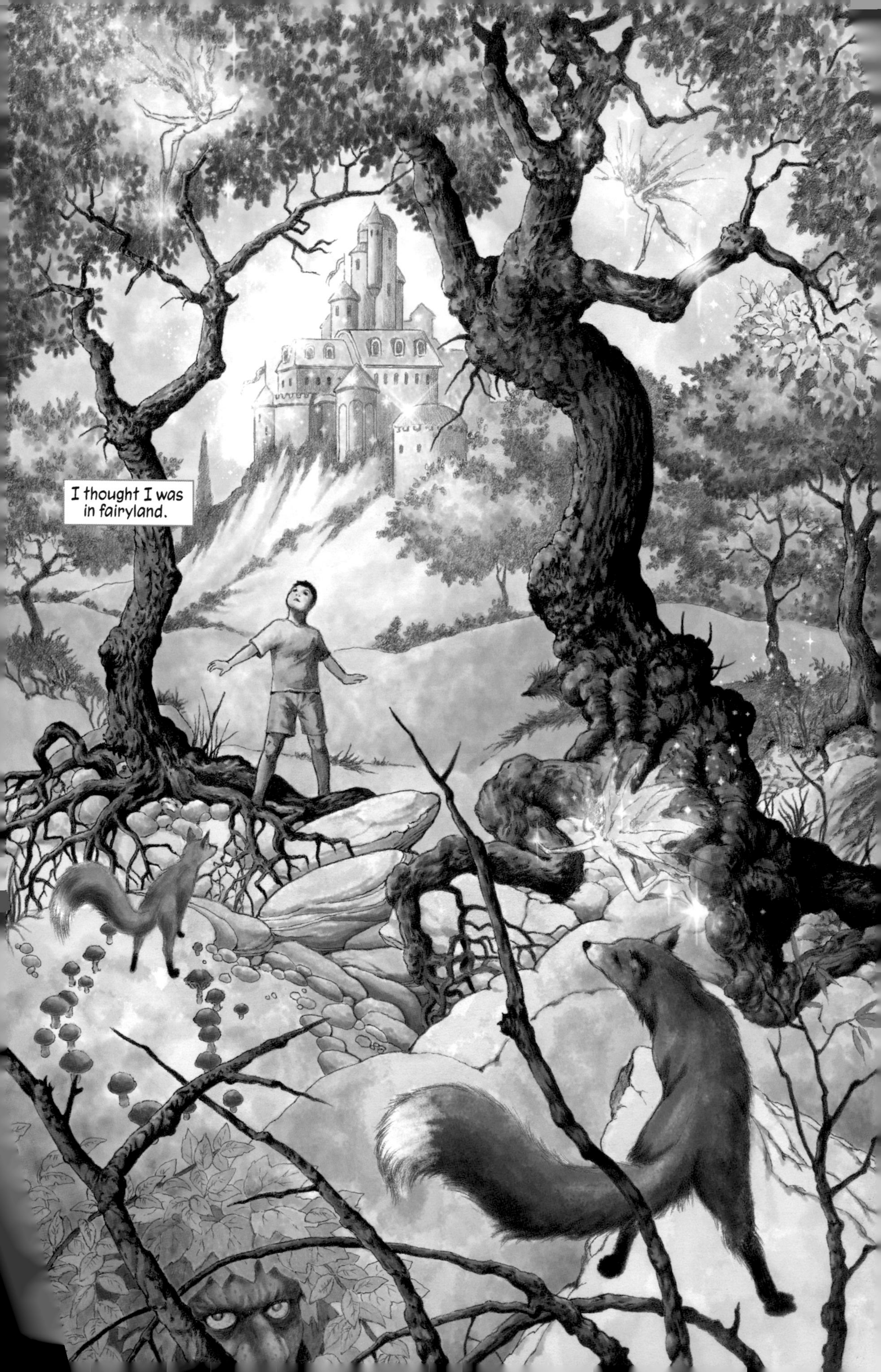
I thought I was in fairyland.

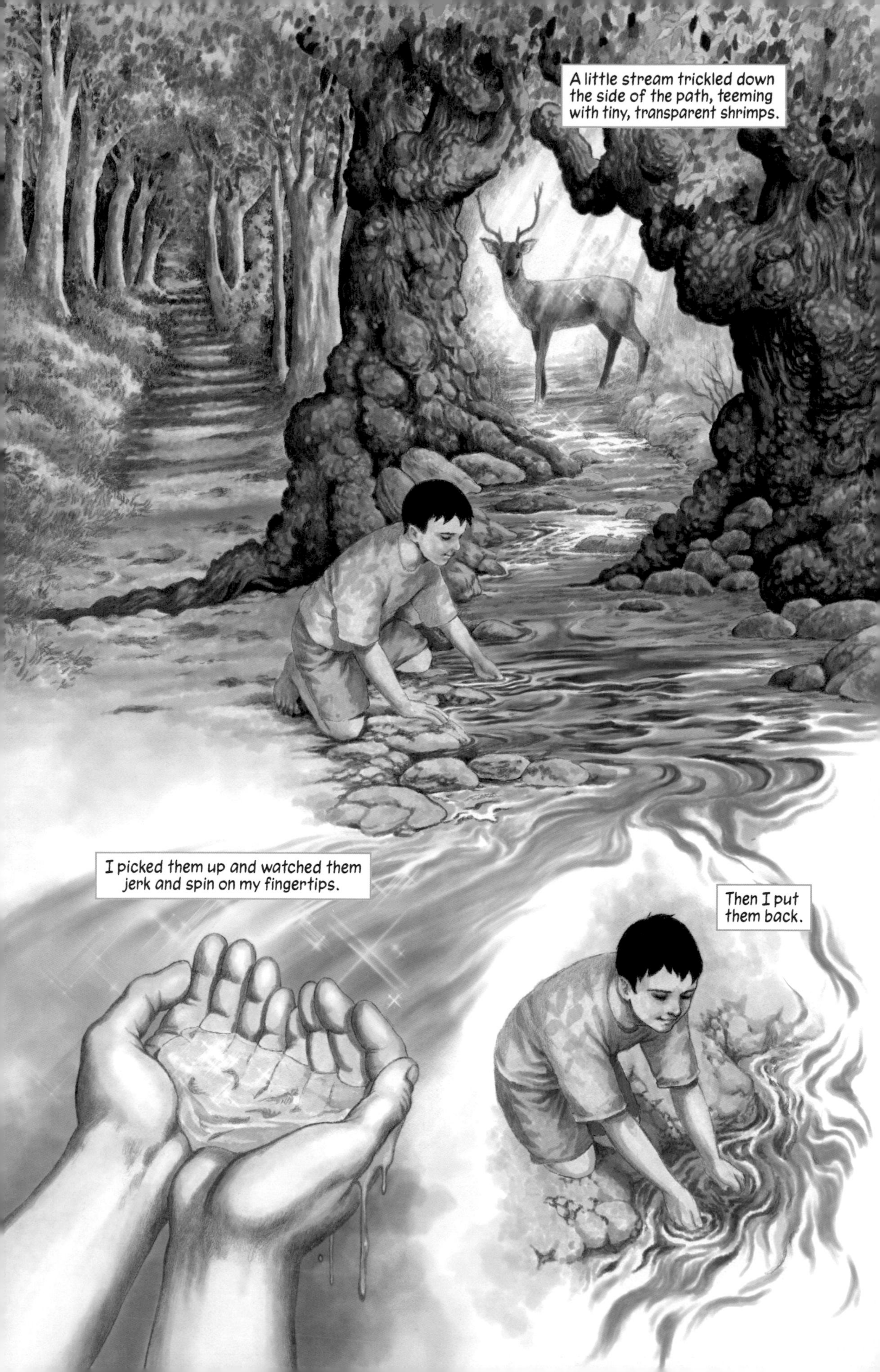
A little stream trickled down the side of the path, teeming with tiny, transparent shrimps.
I picked them up and watched them jerk and spin on my fingertips.
Then I put them back.

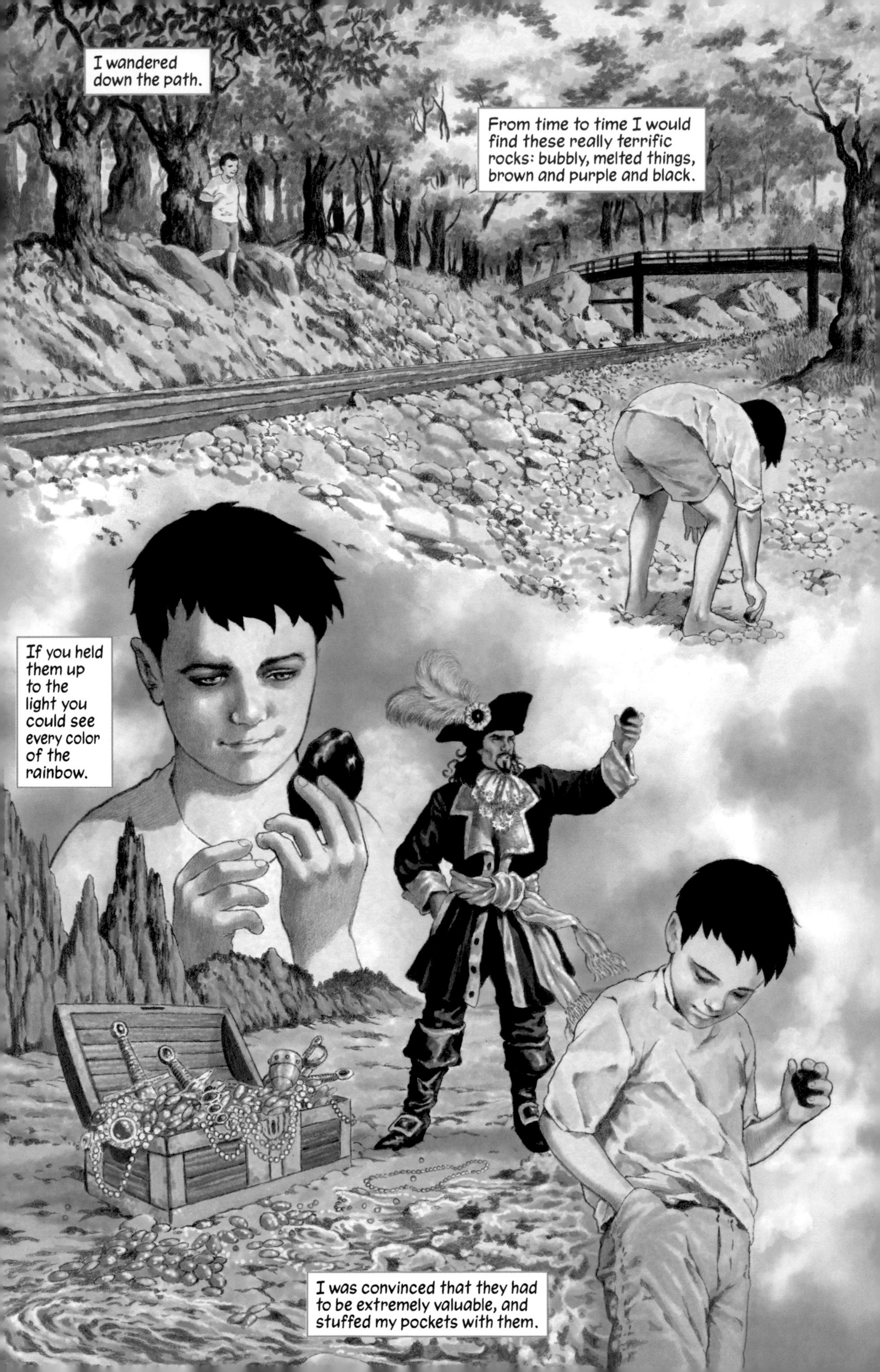
I wandered down the path.
From time to time I would find these really terrific rocks: bubbly, melted things, brown and purple and black.
If you held them up to the light you could see every color of the rainbow.
I was convinced that they had to be extremely valuable, and stuffed my pockets with them.

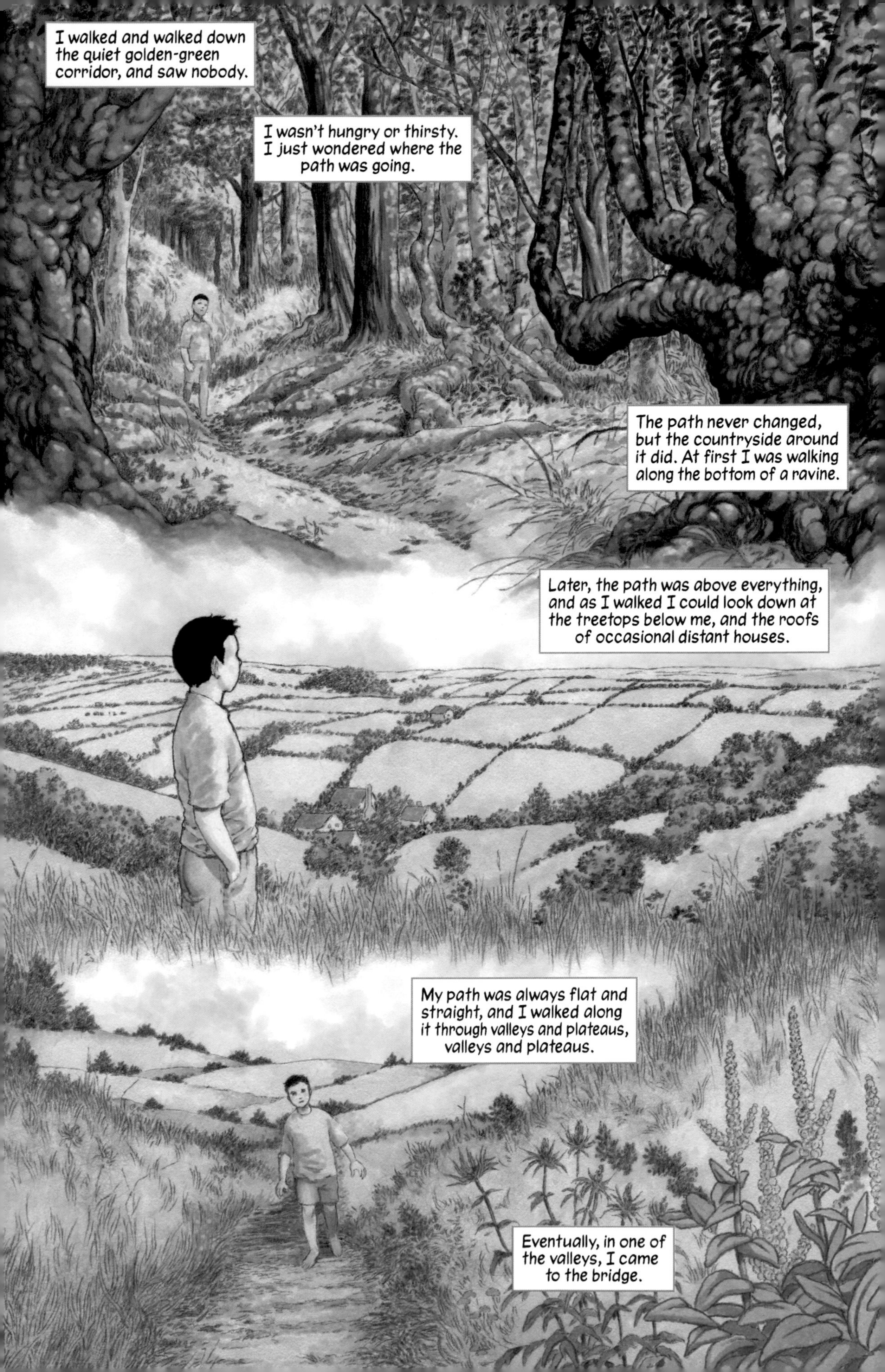
I walked and walked down the quiet golden-green corridor, and saw nobody.
I wasn't hungry or thirsty. I just wondered where the path was going.
The path never changed, but the countryside around it did. At first I was walking along the bottom of a ravine.
Later, the path was above everything, and as I walked I could look down at the treetops below me, and the roofs of occasional distant houses.
My path was always flat and straight, and I walked along it through valleys and plateaus, valleys and plateaus.
Eventually, in one of the valleys, I came to the bridge.

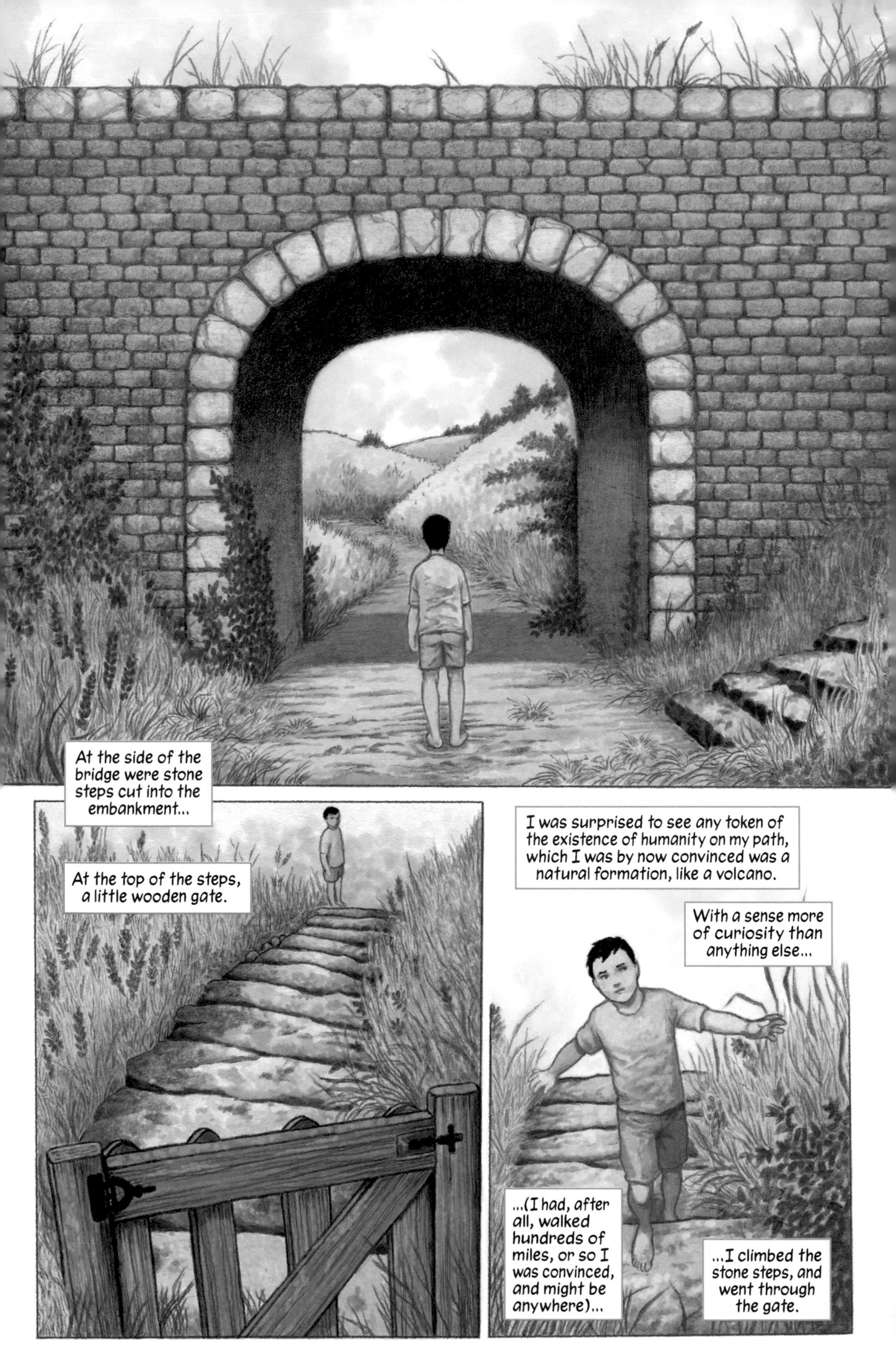
At the side of the bridge were stone steps cut into the embankment...
At the top of the steps, a little wooden gate.
I was surprised to see any token of the existence of humanity on my path, which I was by now convinced was a natural formation, like a volcano.
With a sense more of curiosity than anything else...
...(I had, after all, walked hundreds of miles, or so I was convinced, and might be anywhere)...
...I climbed the stone steps, and went through the gate.

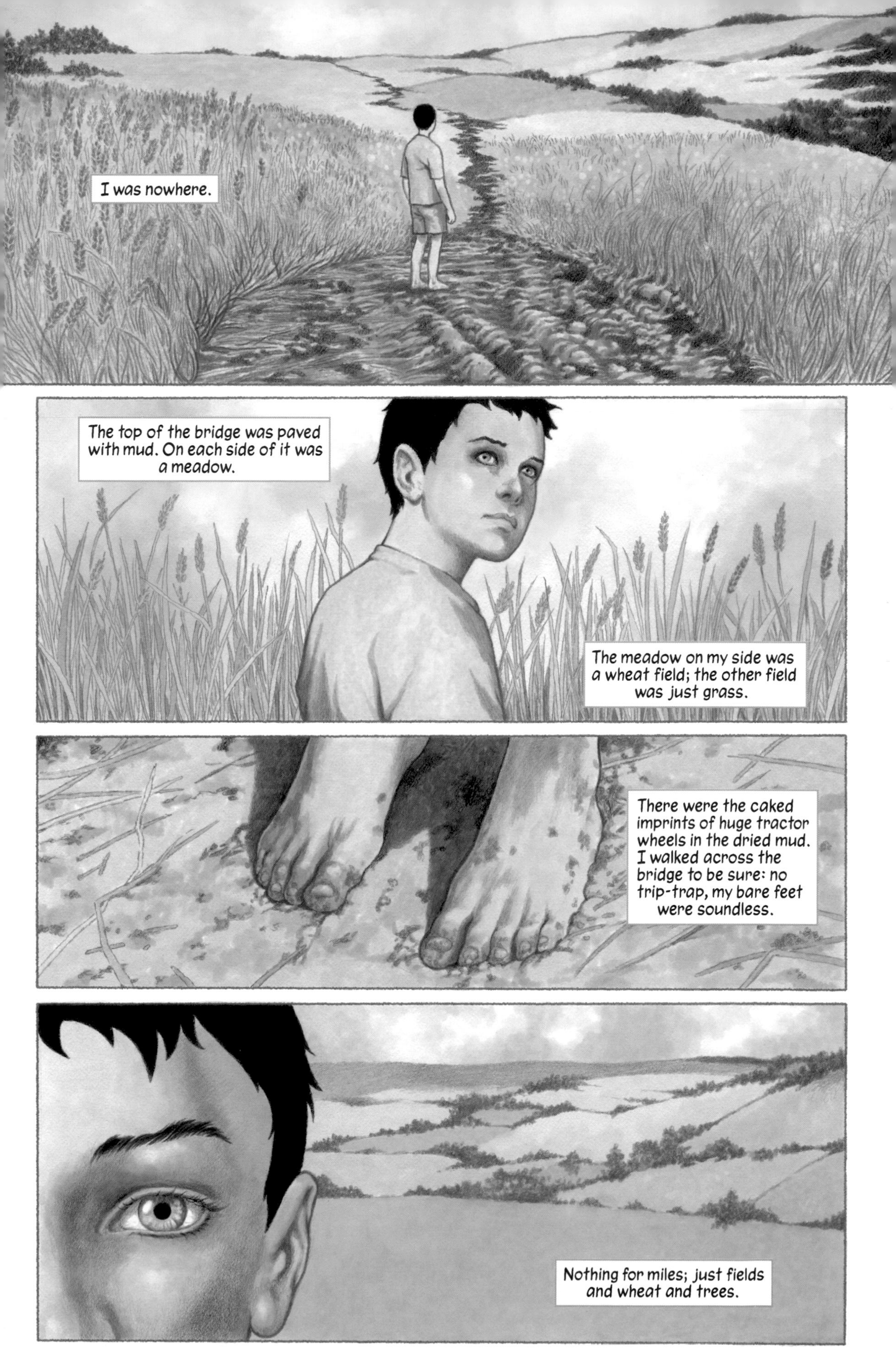
I was nowhere.
The top of the bridge was paved with mud. On each side of it was a meadow.
The meadow on my side was a wheat field; the other field was just grass.
There were the caked imprints of huge tractor wheels in the dried mud. I walked across the bridge to be sure: no trip-trap, my bare feet were soundless.
Nothing for miles; just fields and wheat and trees.

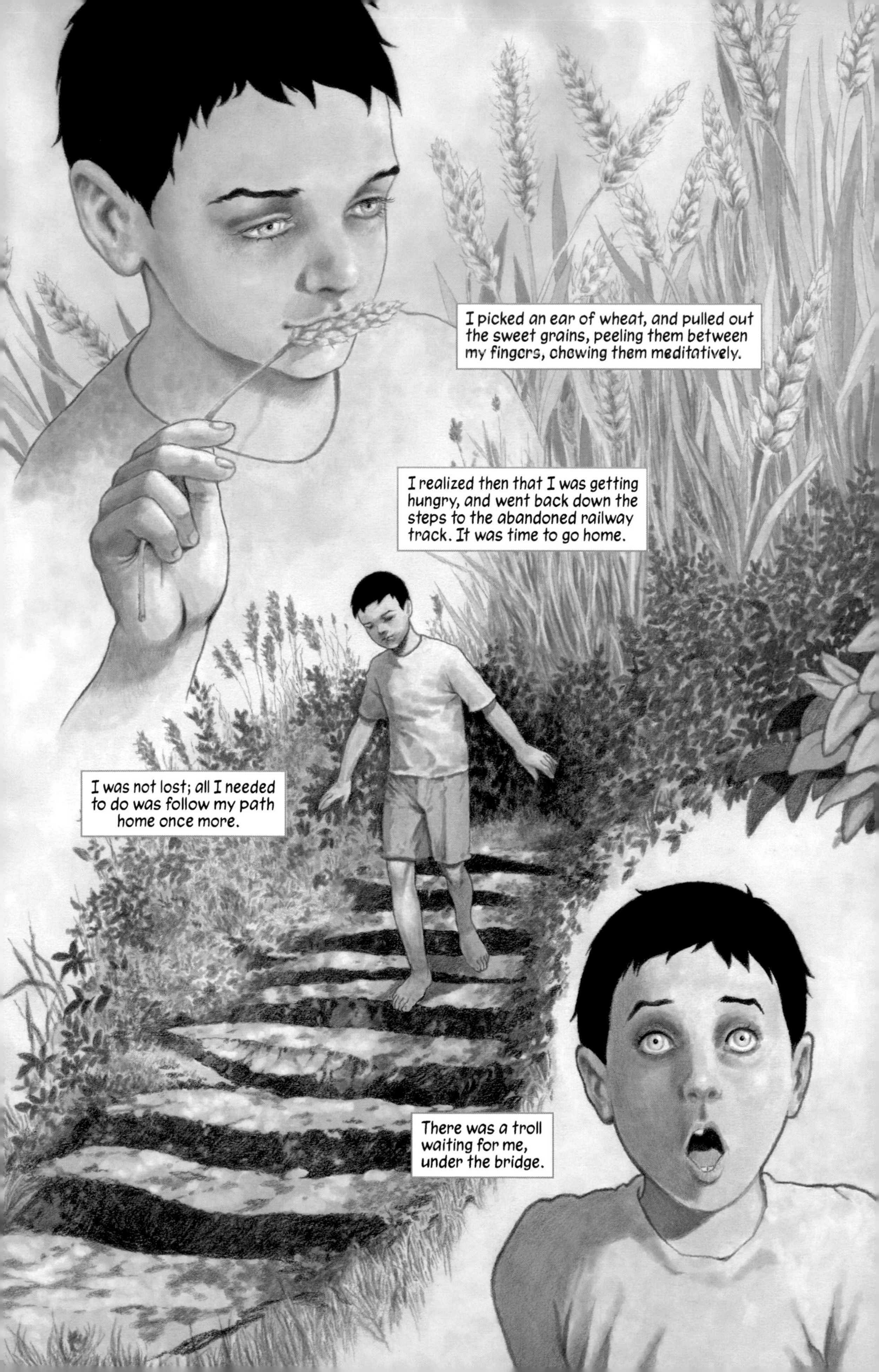
I picked an ear of wheat, and pulled out the sweet grains, peeling them between my fingers, chewing them meditatively.
I realized then that I was getting hungry, and went back down the steps to the abandoned railway track. It was time to go home.
I was not lost; all I needed to do was follow my path home once more.
There was a troll waiting for me, under the bridge.

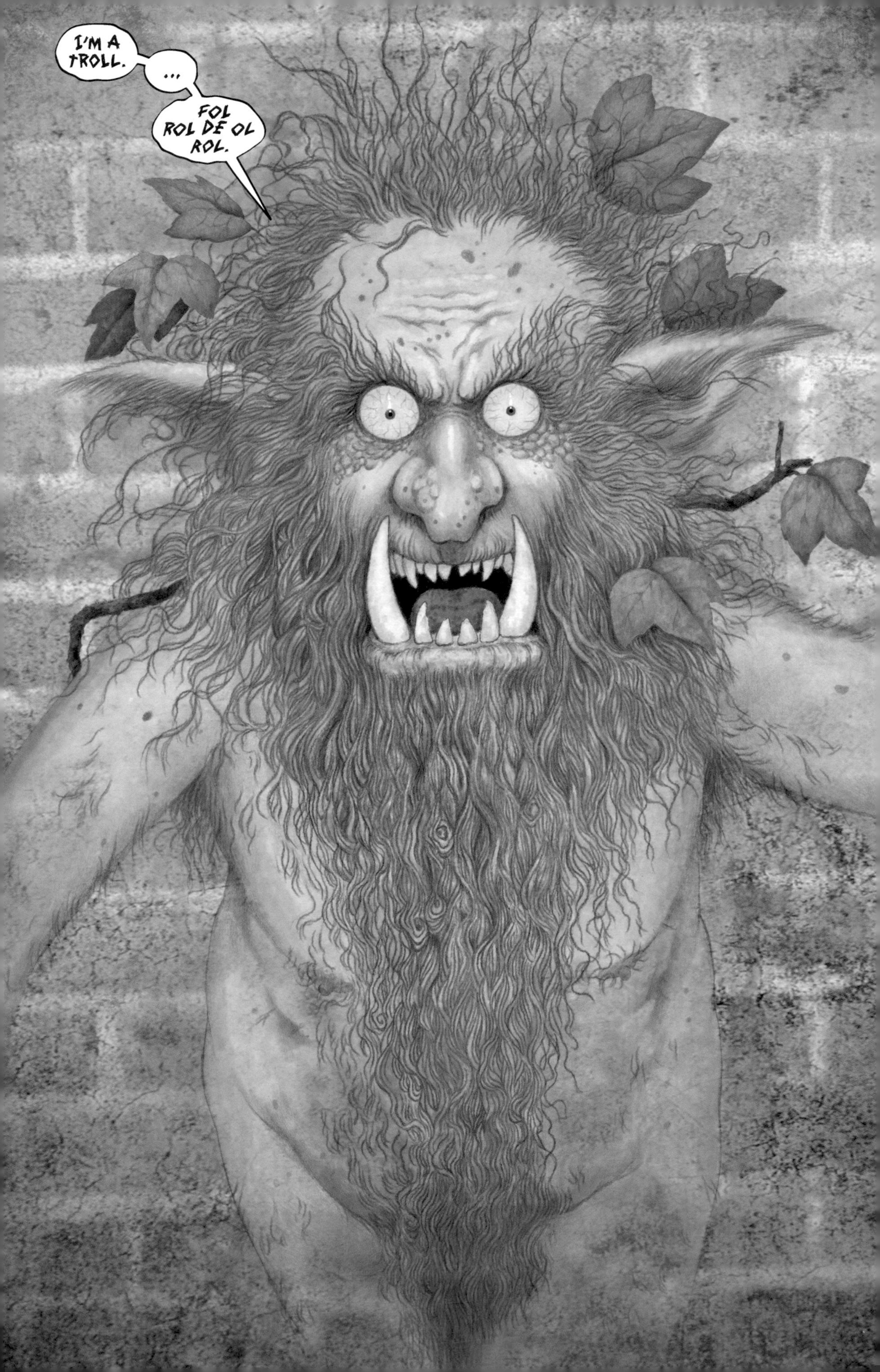
I'M A TROLL.
...
FOL ROL DE OL ROL.

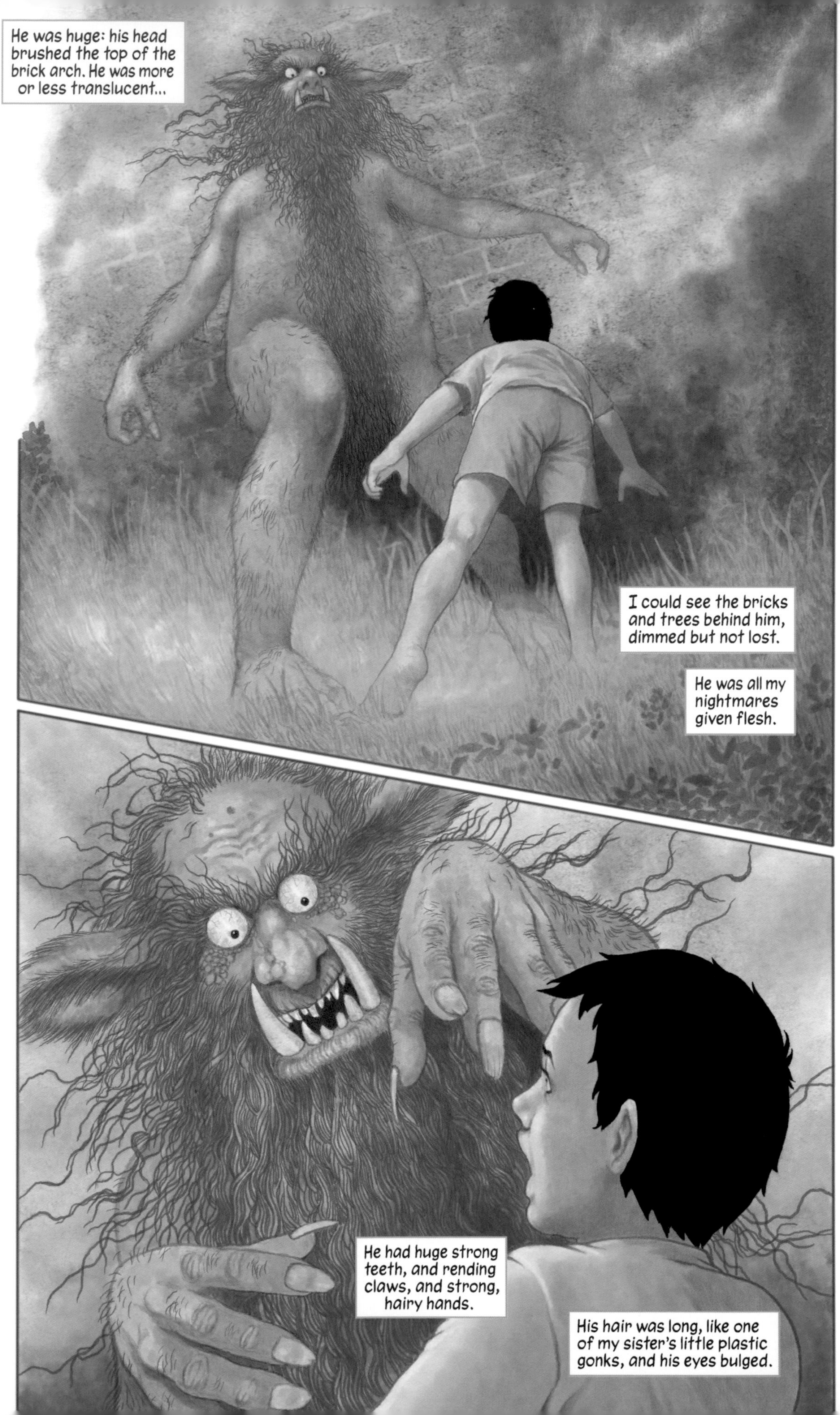
He was huge: his head brushed the top of the brick arch. He was more or less translucent...
I could see the bricks and trees behind him, dimmed but not lost.
He was all my nightmares given flesh.
He had huge strong teeth, and rending claws, and strong, hairy hands.
His hair was long, like one of my sister's little plastic gonks, and his eyes bulged.

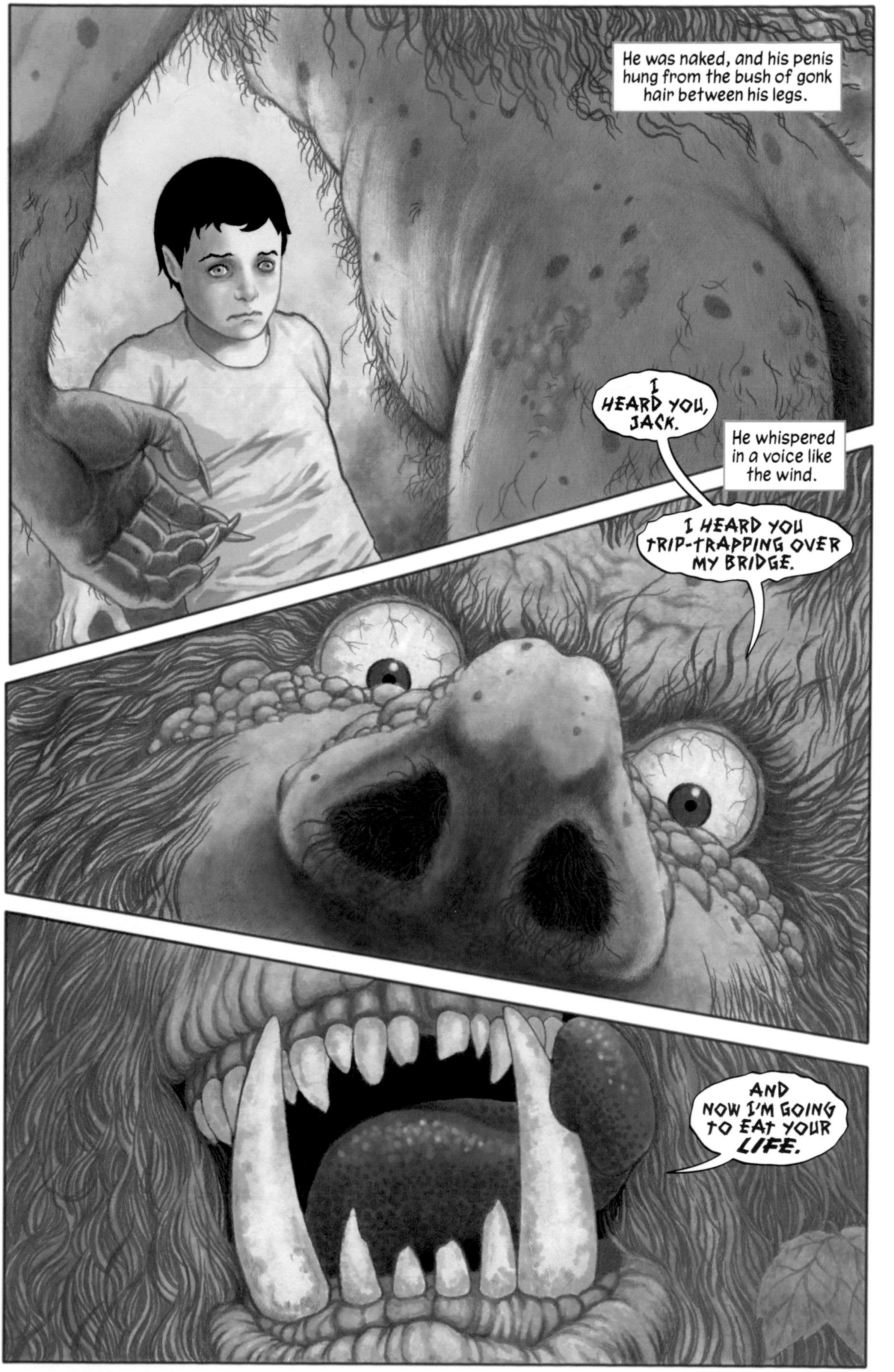
He was naked, and his penis hung from the bush of gonk hair between his legs.
I HEARD YOU, JACK.
He whispered in a voice like the wind.
I HEARD YOU TRIP-TRAPPING OVER MY BRIDGE.
AND NOW I'M GOING TO EAT YOUR LIFE.

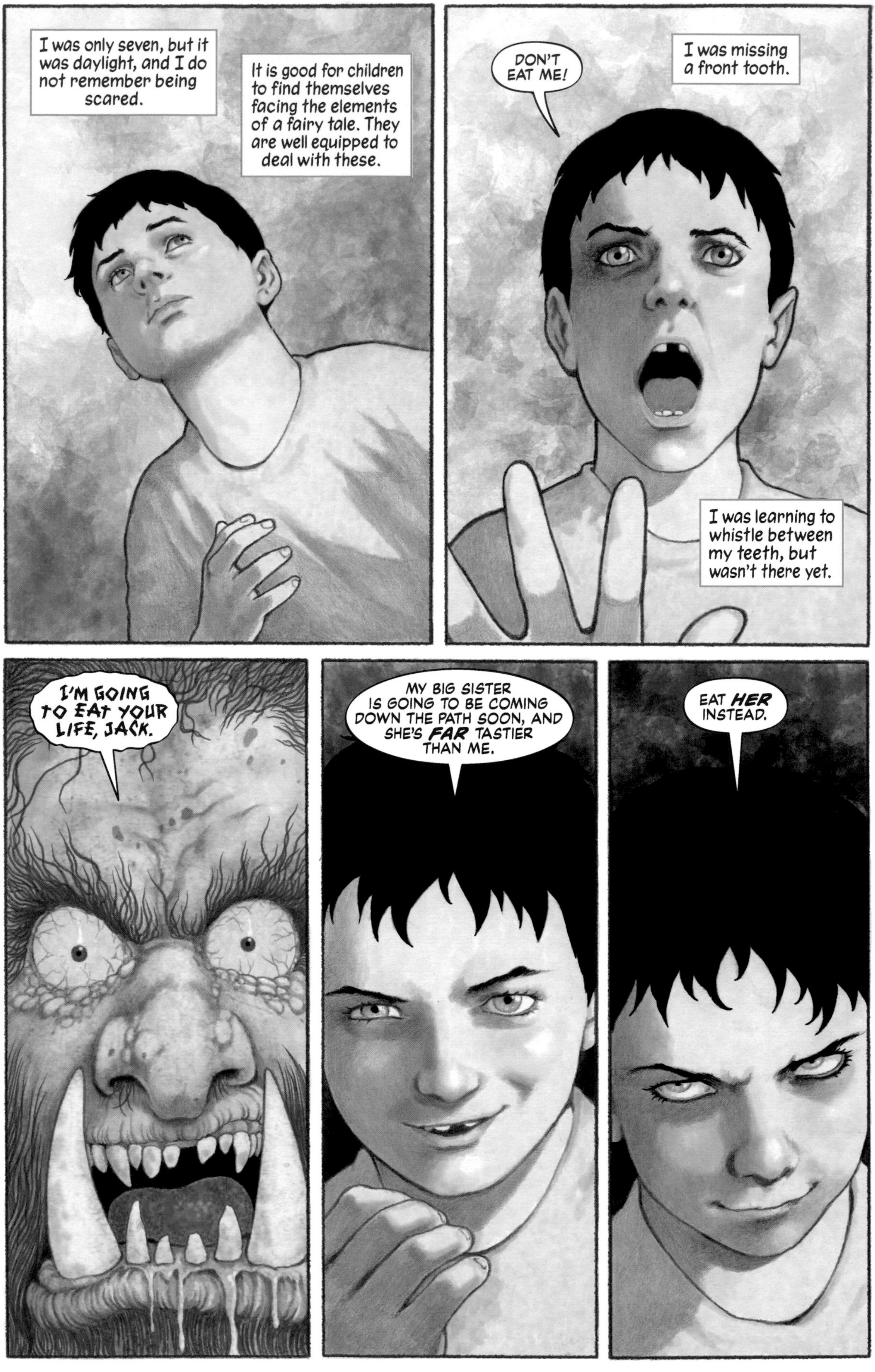
I was only seven, but it was daylight, and I do not remember being scared.
It is good for children to find themselves facing the elements of a fairy tale. They are well equipped to deal with these.
DON'T EAT ME!
I was missing a front tooth.
I was learning to whistle between my teeth, but wasn't there yet.
I'M GOING TO EAT YOUR LIFE, JACK.
MY BIG SISTER IS GOING TO BE COMING DOWN THE PATH SOON, AND SHE'S FAR TASTIER THAN ME.
EAT HER INSTEAD.

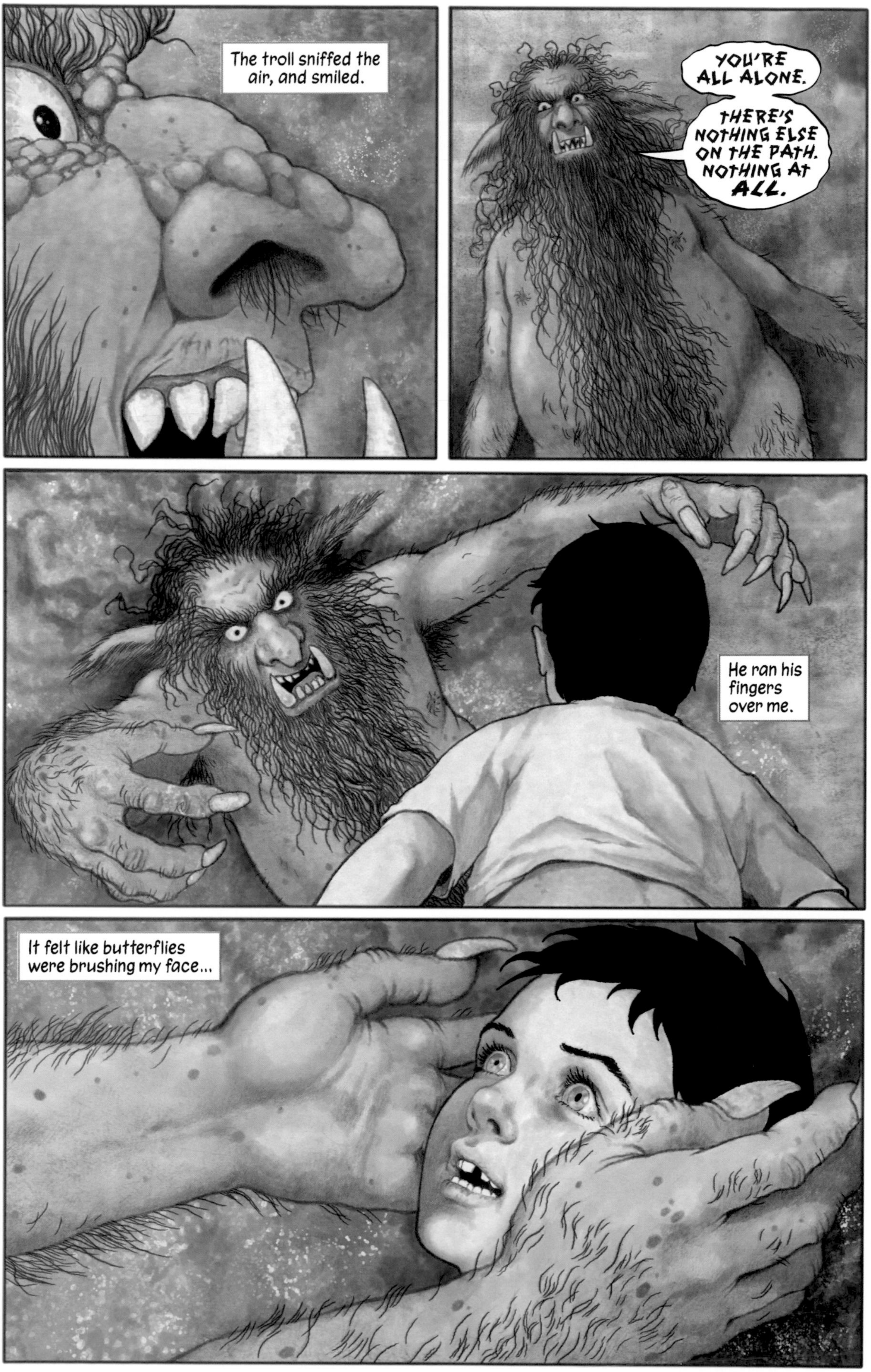

The troll sniffed the air, and smiled.
YOU'RE ALL ALONE.
THERE'S NOTHING ELSE ON THE PATH. NOTHING AT ALL.
He ran his fingers over me.
It felt like butterflies were brushing my face...

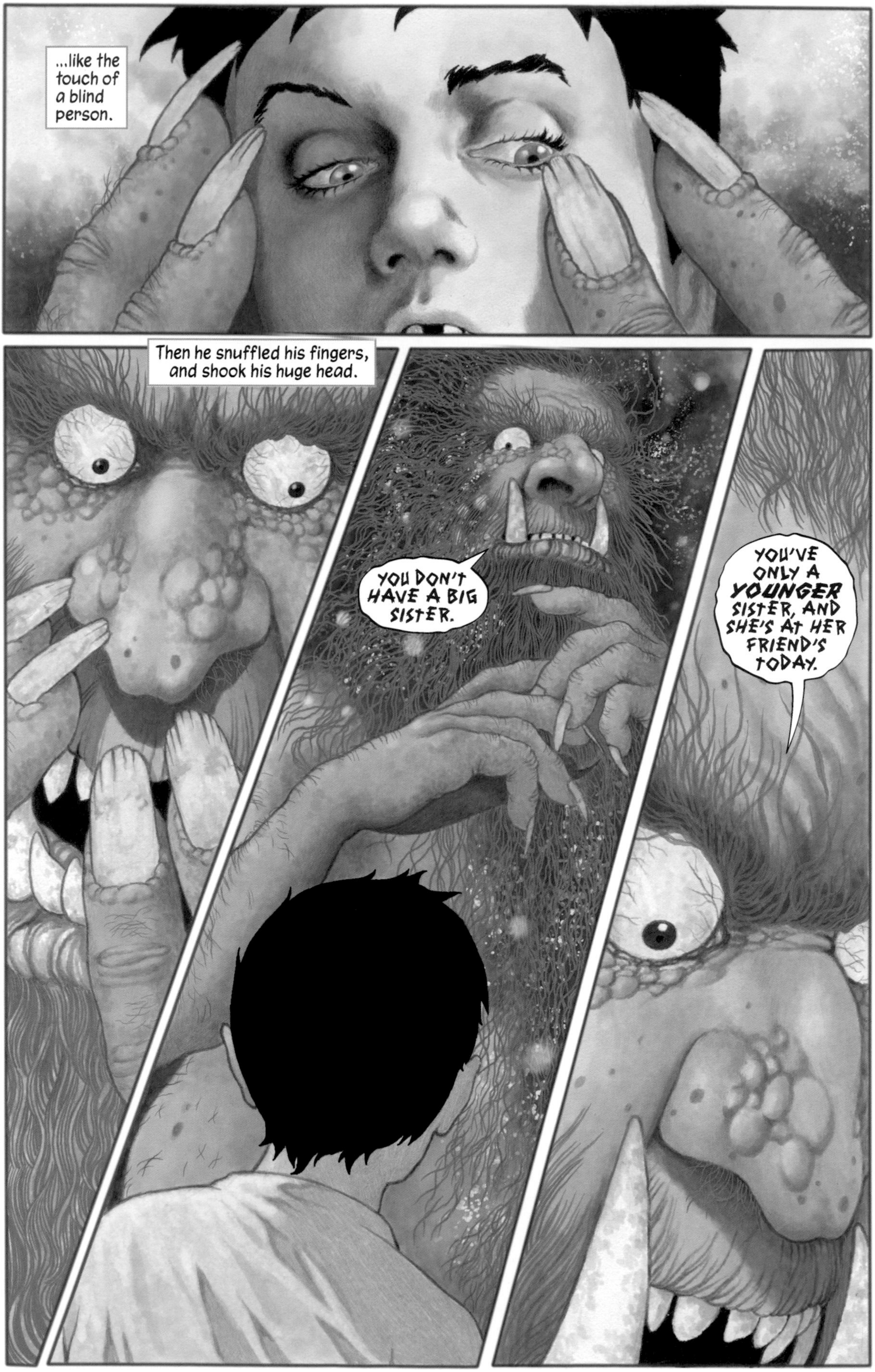
...like the touch of a blind person.
Then he snuffled his fingers, and shook his huge head.
YOU DON'T HAVE A BIG SISTER.
YOU'VE ONLY A ***YOUNGER*** SISTER, AND SHE'S AT HER FRIEND'S TODAY.

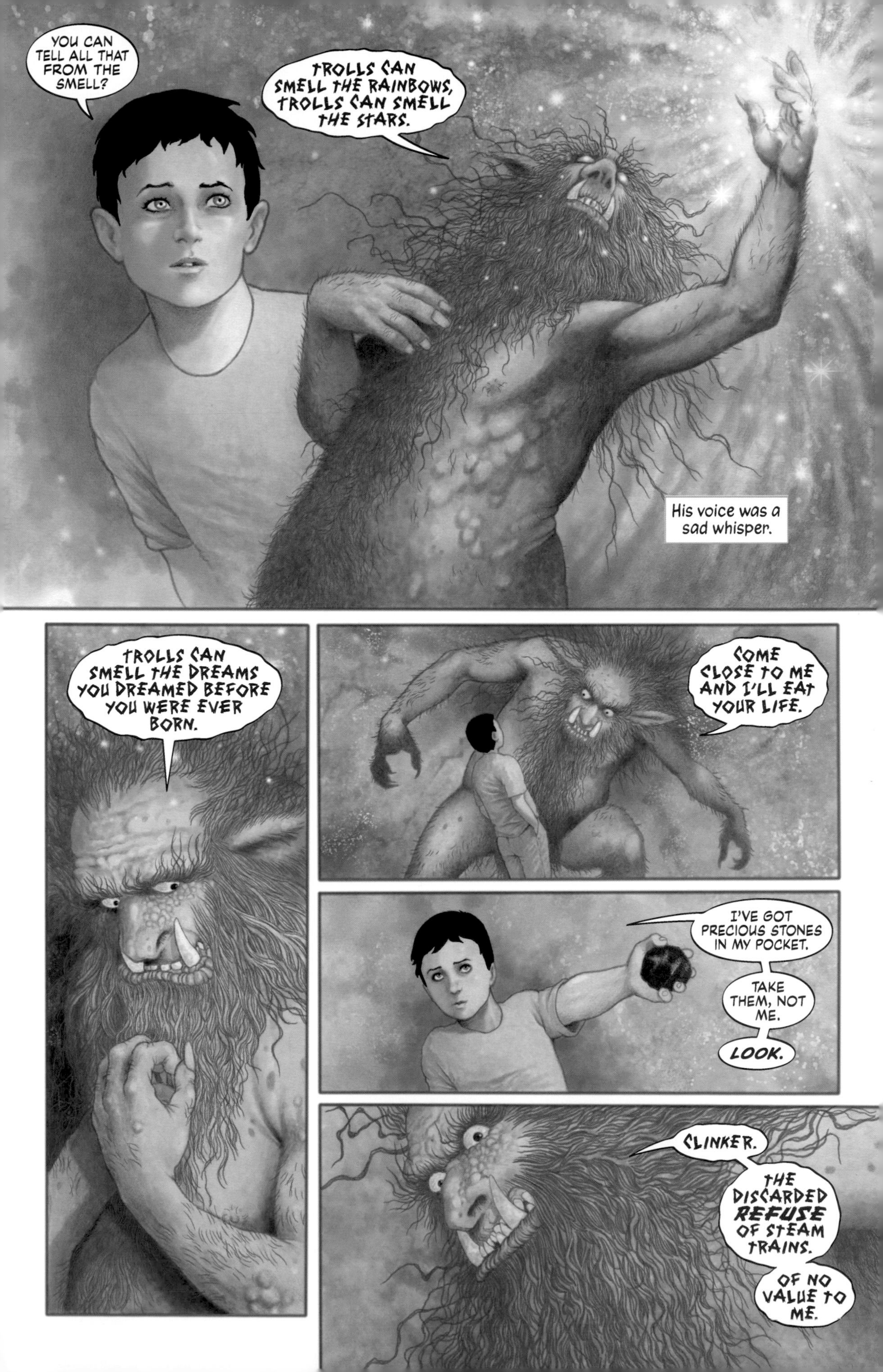
YOU CAN TELL ALL THAT FROM THE SMELL?
TROLLS CAN SMELL THE RAINBOWS, TROLLS CAN SMELL THE STARS.
His voice was a sad whisper.
TROLLS CAN SMELL THE DREAMS YOU DREAMED BEFORE YOU WERE EVER BORN.
COME CLOSE TO ME AND I'LL EAT YOUR LIFE.
I'VE GOT PRECIOUS STONES IN MY POCKET.
TAKE THEM, NOT ME.
LOOK.
CLINKER.
THE DISCARDED REFUSE OF STEAM TRAINS.
OF NO VALUE TO ME.

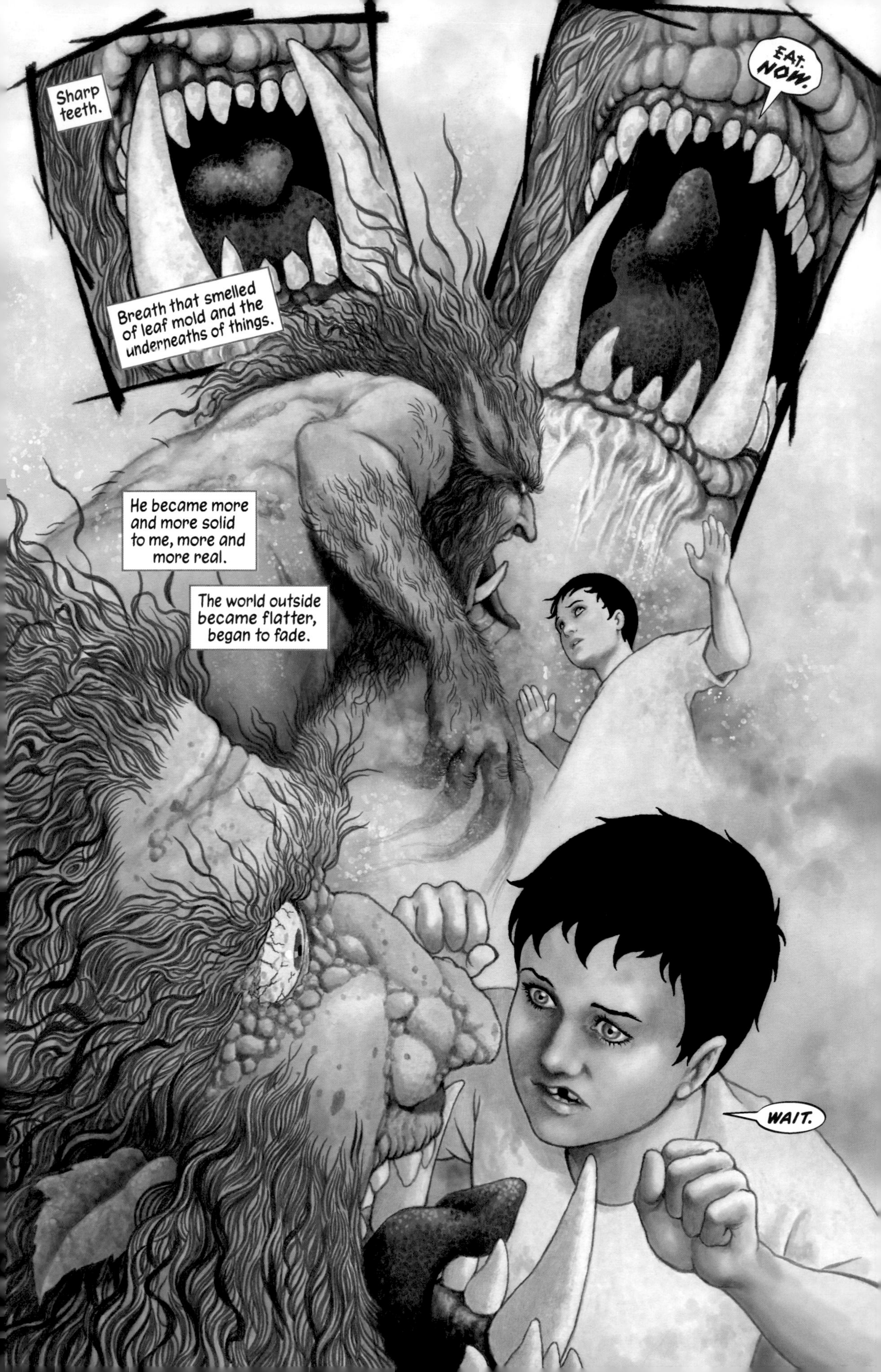
Sharp teeth.
EAT. NOW.
Breath that smelled of leaf mold and the underneaths of things.
He became more and more solid to me, more and more real.
The world outside became flatter, began to fade.
WAIT.

I dug my feet into the damp earth beneath the bridge, wiggled my toes, held on tightly to the real world.

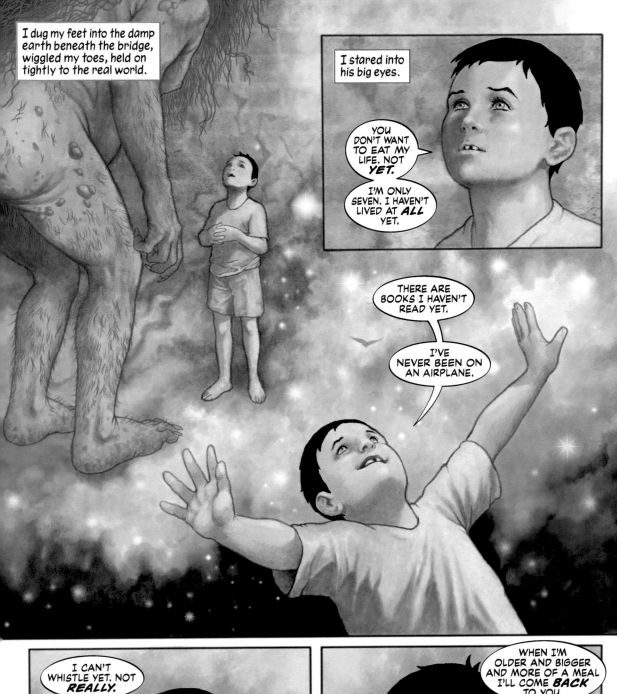

I stared into his big eyes.

YOU DON'T WANT TO EAT MY LIFE. NOT YET.

I'M ONLY SEVEN. I HAVEN'T LIVED AT ALL YET.

THERE ARE BOOKS I HAVEN'T READ YET.

I'VE NEVER BEEN ON AN AIRPLANE.

I CAN'T WHISTLE YET. NOT REALLY.

WHY DON'T YOU LET ME GO?

WHEN I'M OLDER AND BIGGER AND MORE OF A MEAL I'LL COME BACK TO YOU.

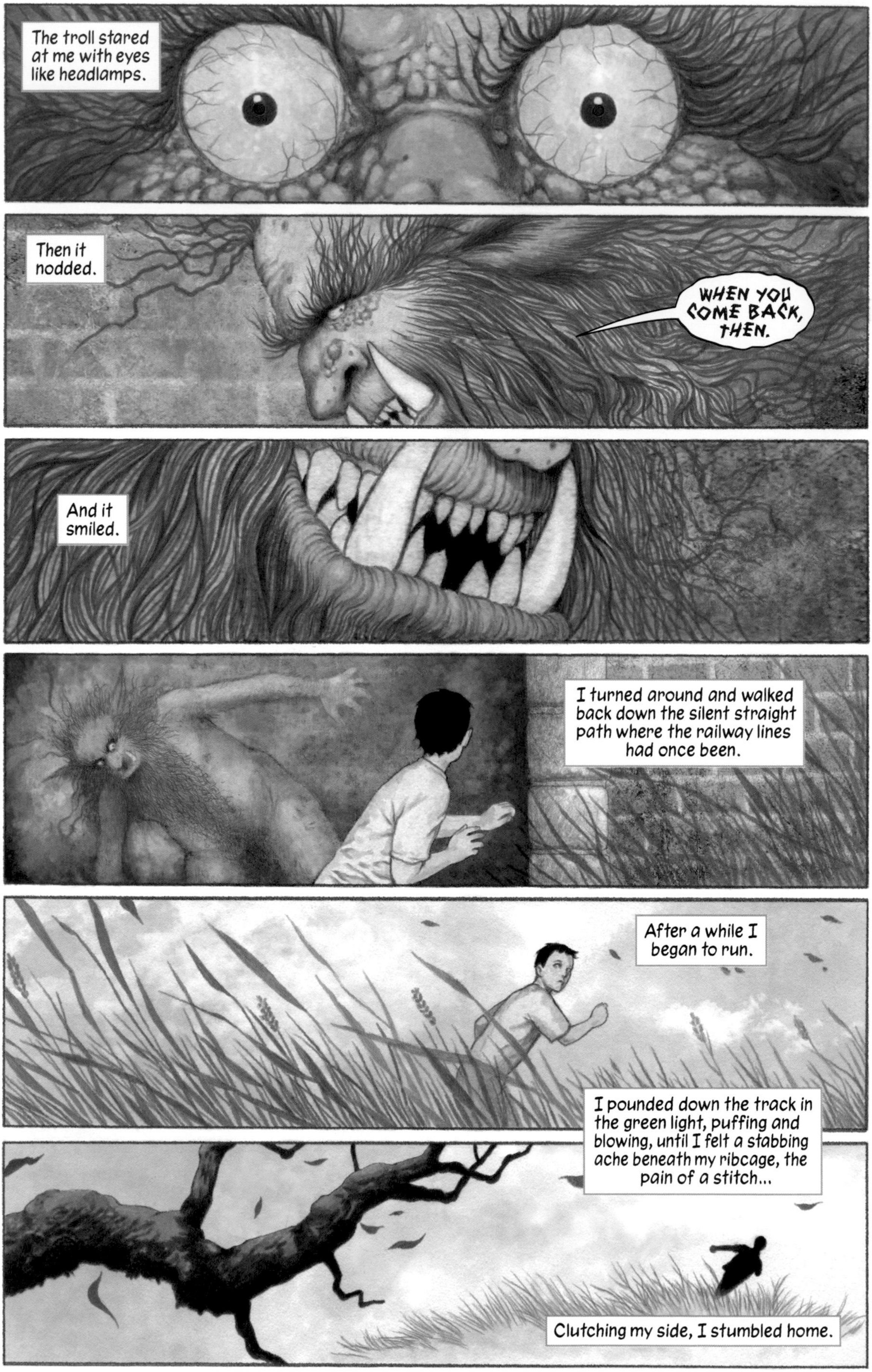
The troll stared at me with eyes like headlamps.
Then it nodded.
WHEN YOU COME BACK, THEN.
And it smiled.
I turned around and walked back down the silent straight path where the railway lines had once been.
After a while I began to run.
I pounded down the track in the green light, puffing and blowing, until I felt a stabbing ache beneath my ribcage, the pain of a stitch...
Clutching my side, I stumbled home.

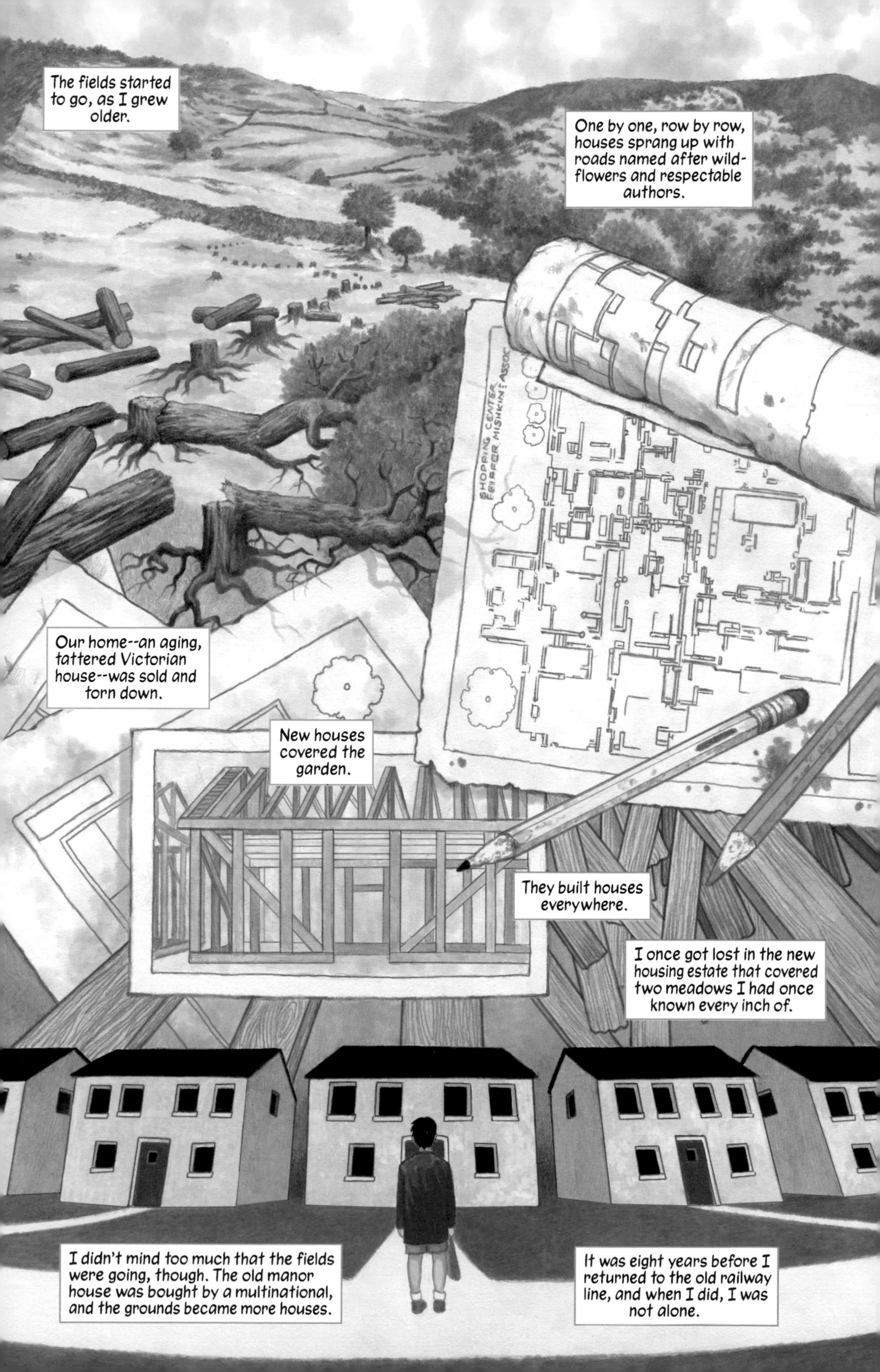
The fields started to go, as I grew older.
One by one, row by row, houses sprang up with roads named after wild-flowers and respectable authors.
SHOPPING CENTER
FEIFFER, MISHKIN & ASSOC
Our home--an aging, tattered Victorian house--was sold and torn down.
New houses covered the garden.
They built houses everywhere.
I once got lost in the new housing estate that covered two meadows I had once known every inch of.
I didn't mind too much that the fields were going, though. The old manor house was bought by a multinational, and the grounds became more houses.
It was eight years before I returned to the old railway line, and when I did, I was not alone.

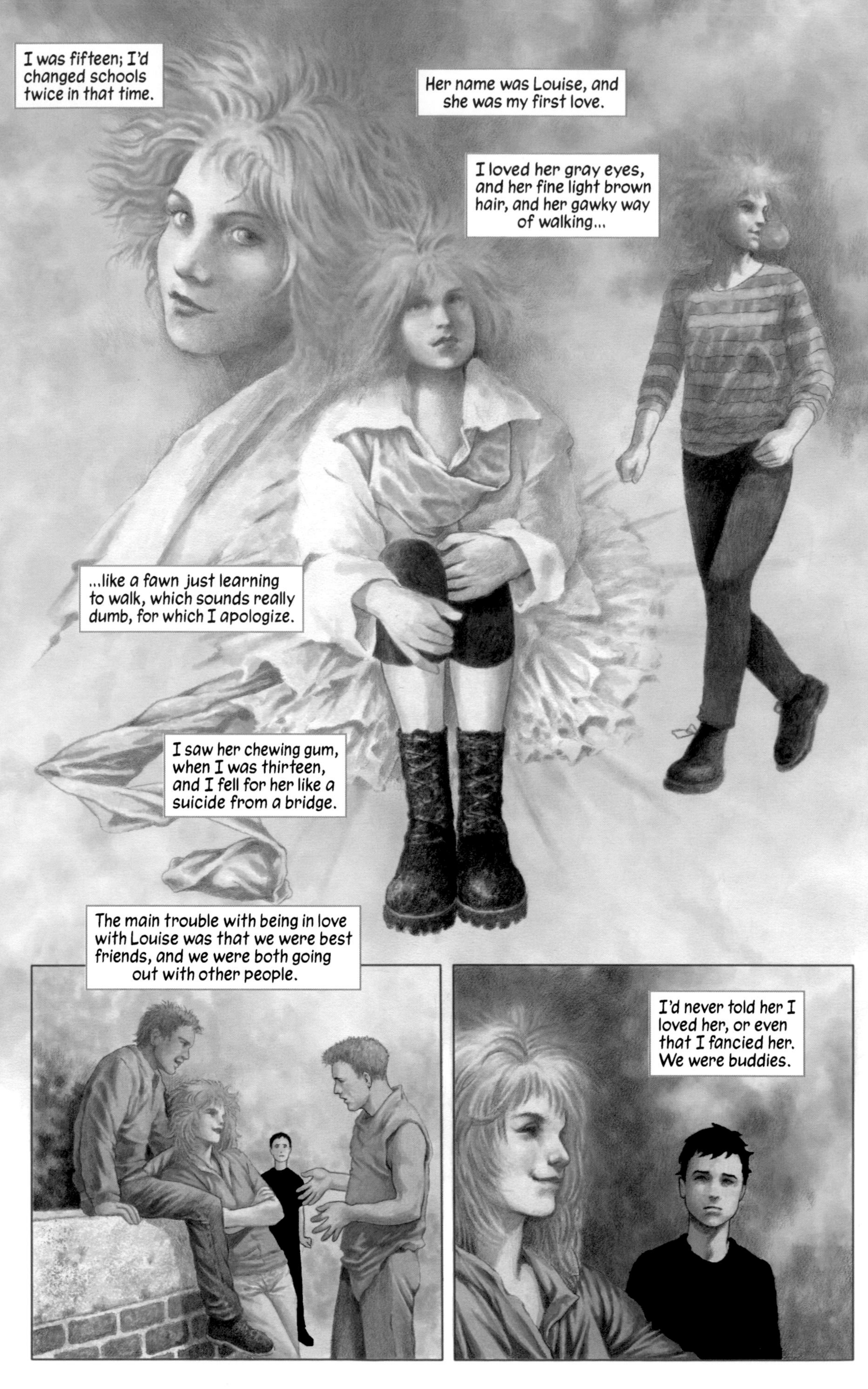
I was fifteen; I'd changed schools twice in that time.
Her name was Louise, and she was my first love.
I loved her gray eyes, and her fine light brown hair, and her gawky way of walking...
...like a fawn just learning to walk, which sounds really dumb, for which I apologize.
I saw her chewing gum, when I was thirteen, and I fell for her like a suicide from a bridge.
The main trouble with being in love with Louise was that we were best friends, and we were both going out with other people.
I'd never told her I loved her, or even that I fancied her. We were buddies.

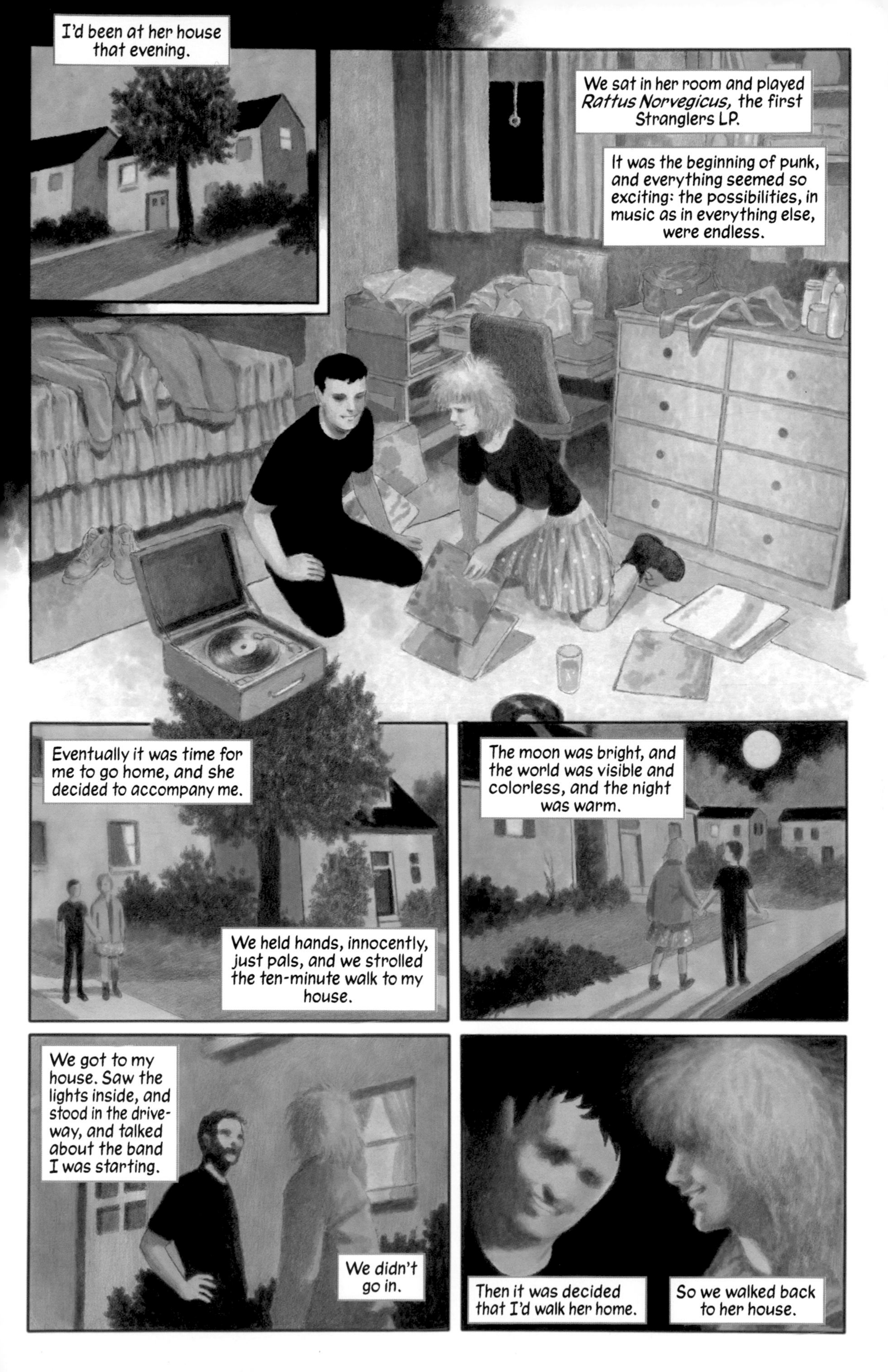

I'd been at her house that evening.
We sat in her room and played *Rattus Norvegicus,* the first Stranglers LP.
It was the beginning of punk, and everything seemed so exciting: the possibilities, in music as in everything else, were endless.
Eventually it was time for me to go home, and she decided to accompany me.
We held hands, innocently, just pals, and we strolled the ten-minute walk to my house.
The moon was bright, and the world was visible and colorless, and the night was warm.
We got to my house. Saw the lights inside, and stood in the drive-way, and talked about the band I was starting.
We didn't go in.
Then it was decided that I'd walk her home.
So we walked back to her house.

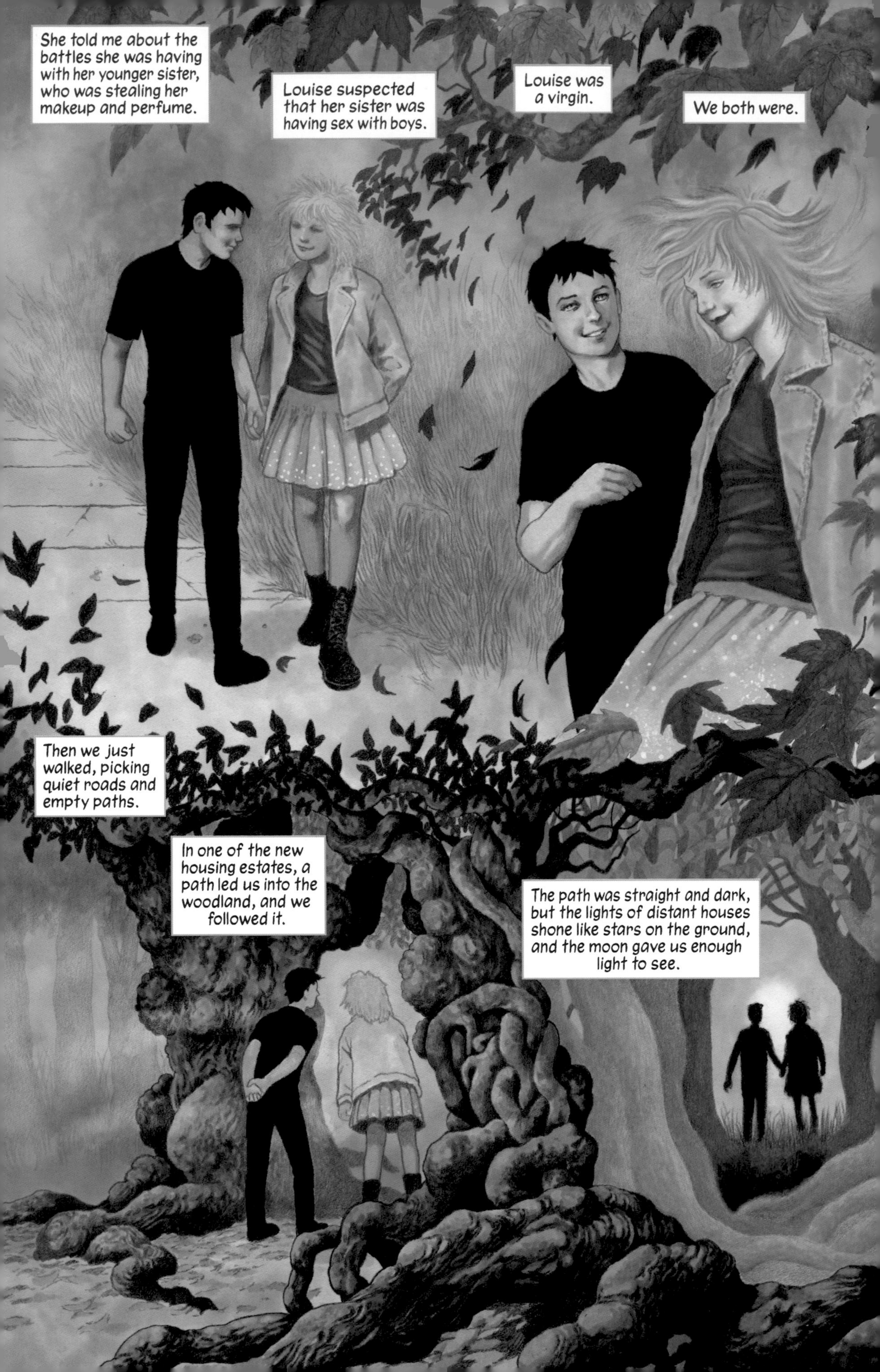
She told me about the battles she was having with her younger sister, who was stealing her makeup and perfume.
Louise suspected that her sister was having sex with boys.
Louise was a virgin.
We both were.
Then we just walked, picking quiet roads and empty paths.
In one of the new housing estates, a path led us into the woodland, and we followed it.
The path was straight and dark, but the lights of distant houses shone like stars on the ground, and the moon gave us enough light to see.

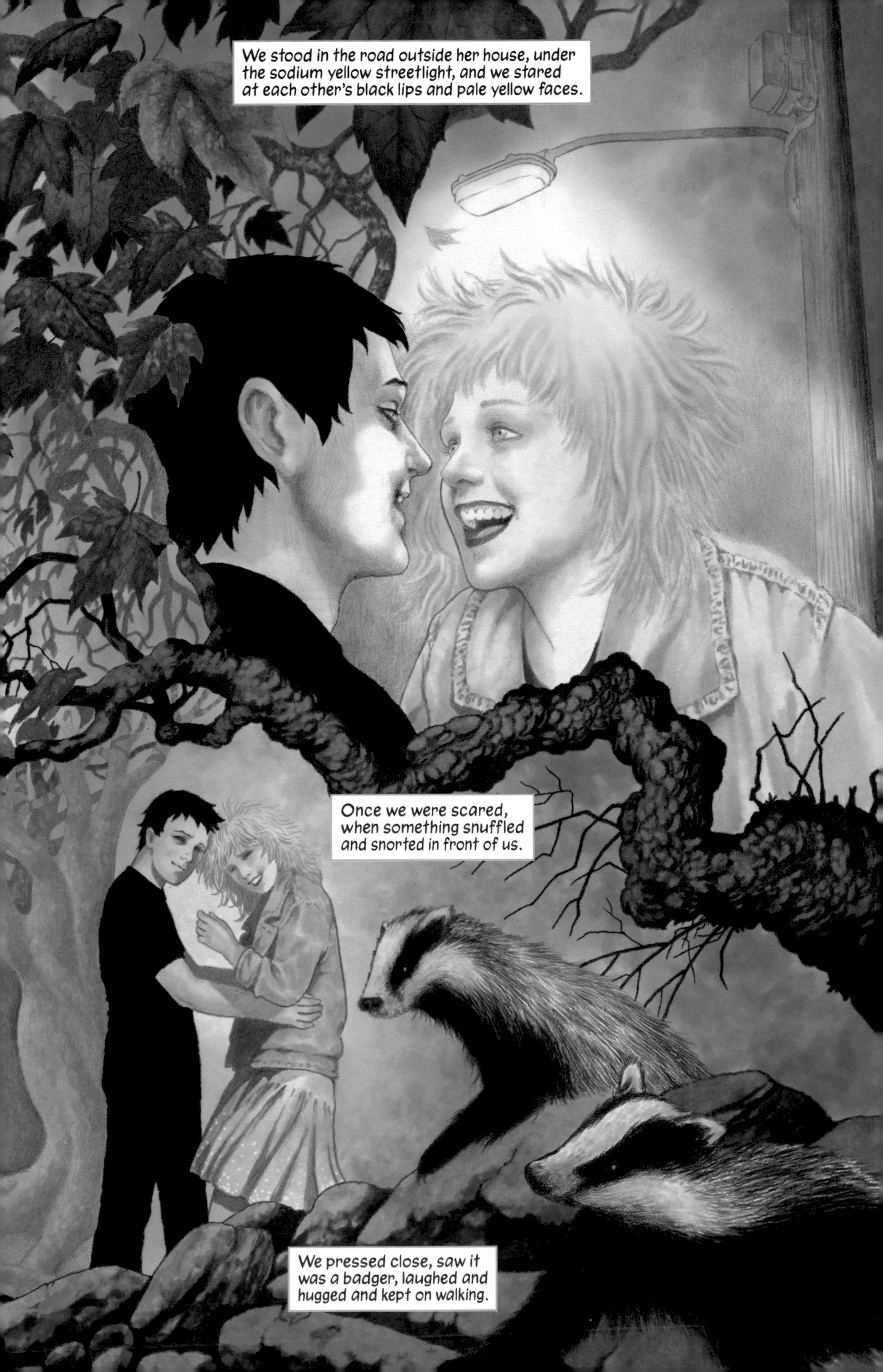
We stood in the road outside her house, under the sodium yellow streetlight, and we stared at each other's black lips and pale yellow faces.
Once we were scared, when something snuffled and snorted in front of us.
We pressed close, saw it was a badger, laughed and hugged and kept on walking.

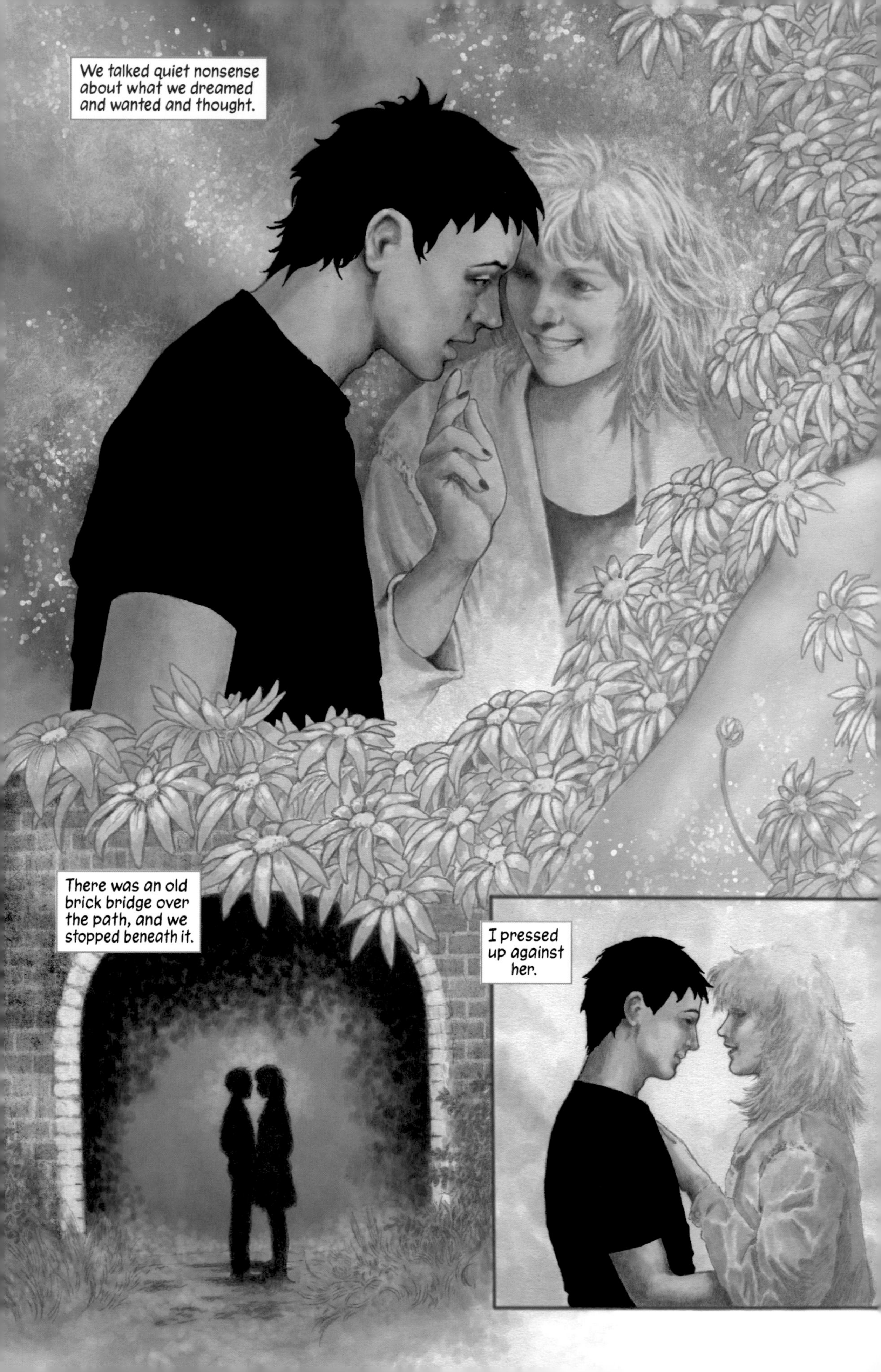
We talked quiet nonsense about what we dreamed and wanted and thought.
There was an old brick bridge over the path, and we stopped beneath it.
I pressed up against her.

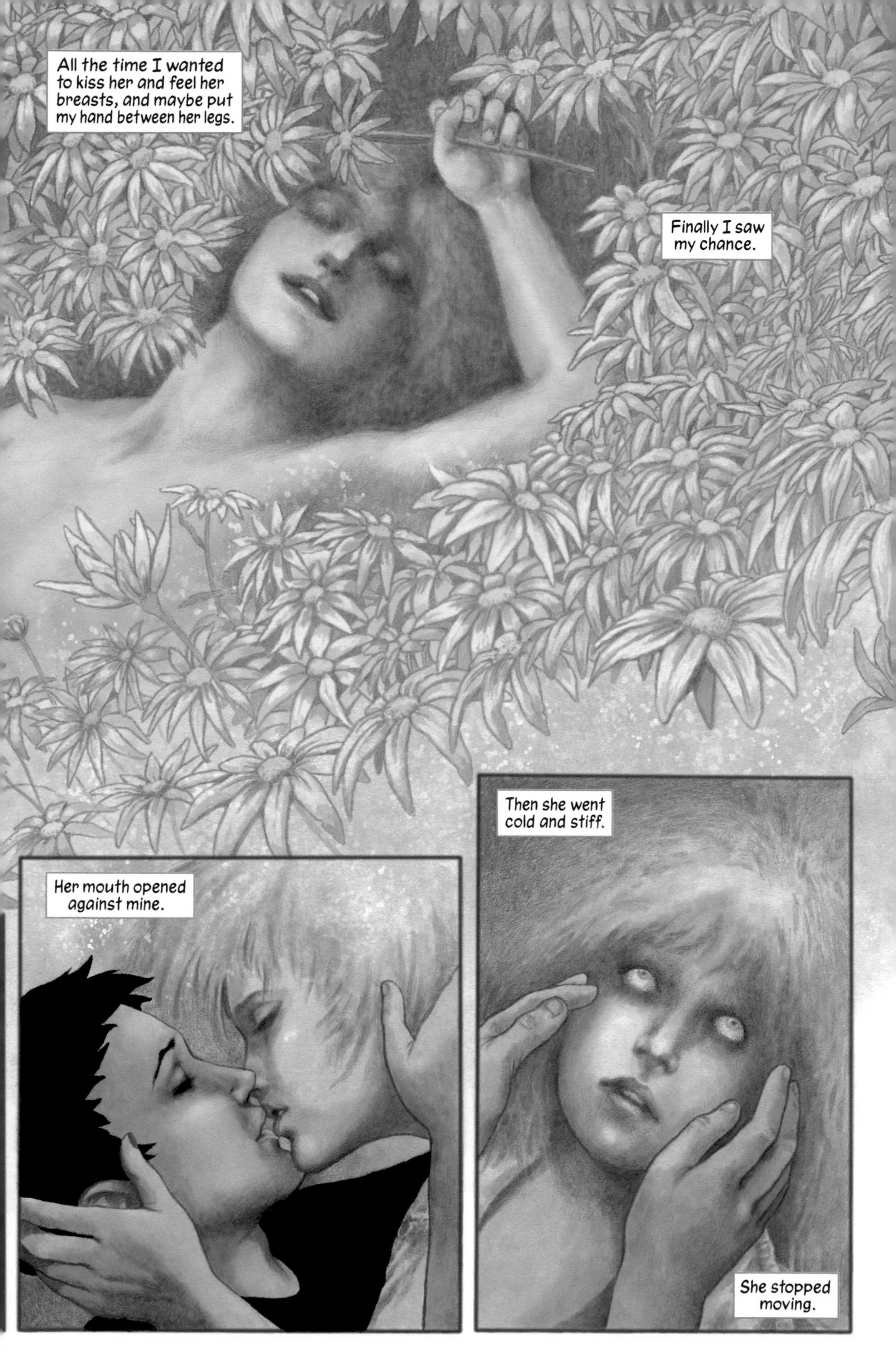
All the time I wanted to kiss her and feel her breasts, and maybe put my hand between her legs.
Finally I saw my chance.
Her mouth opened against mine.
Then she went cold and stiff.
She stopped moving.

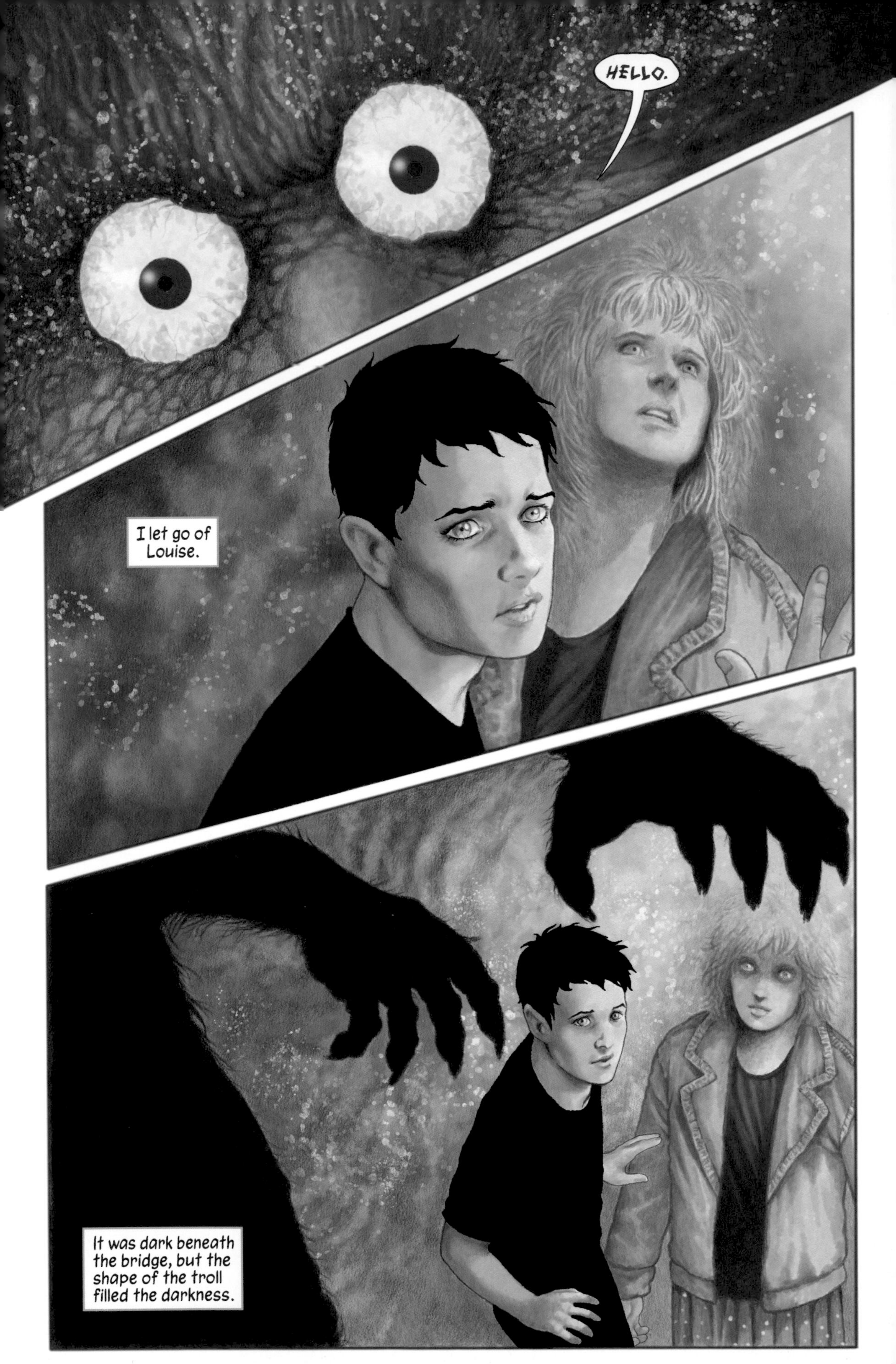
HELLO.
I let go of Louise.
It was dark beneath the bridge, but the shape of the troll filled the darkness.

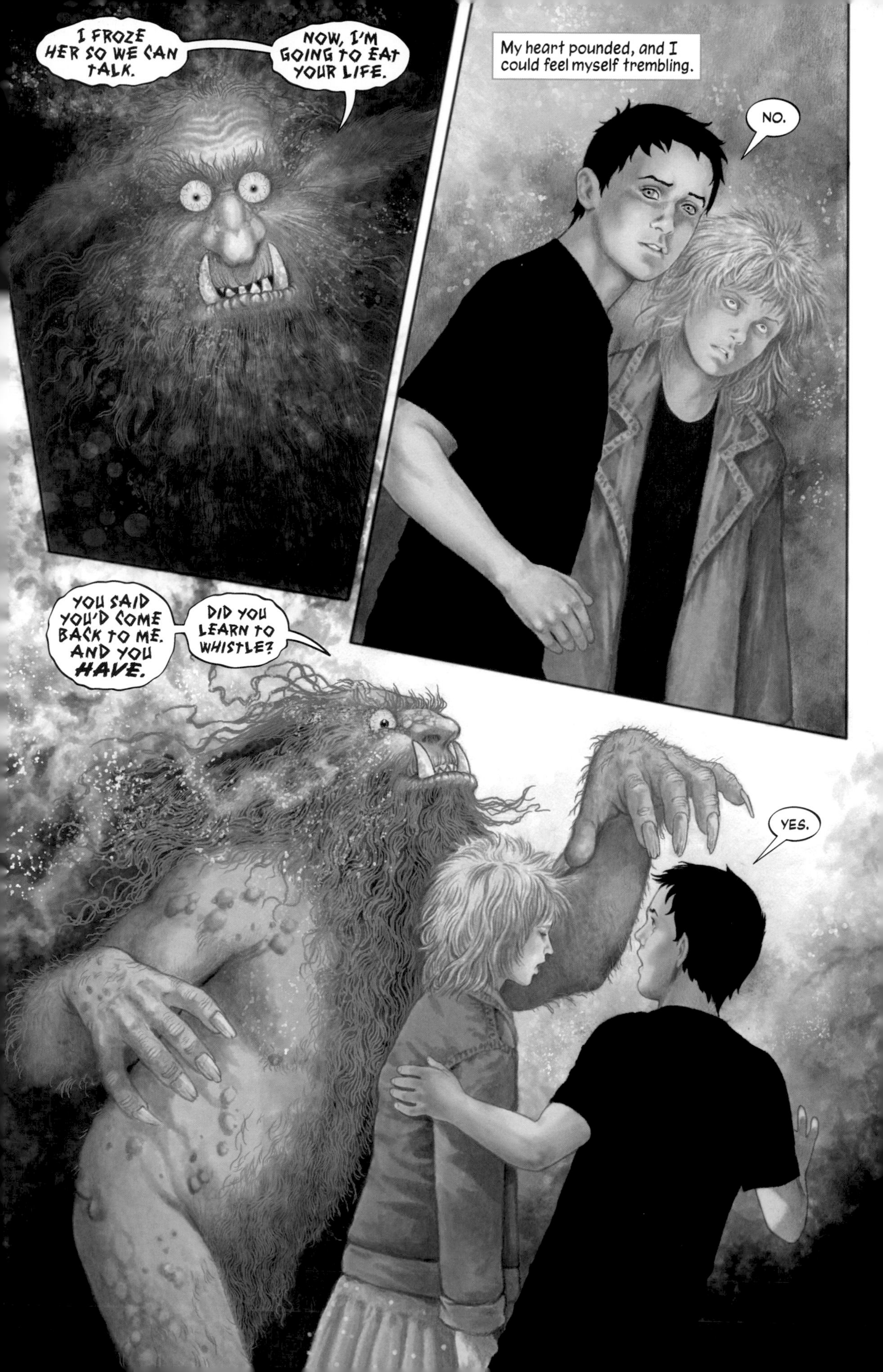

I FROZE HER SO WE CAN TALK.
NOW, I'M GOING TO EAT YOUR LIFE.
My heart pounded, and I could feel myself trembling.
NO.
YOU SAID YOU'D COME BACK TO ME. AND YOU HAVE.
DID YOU LEARN TO WHISTLE?
YES.

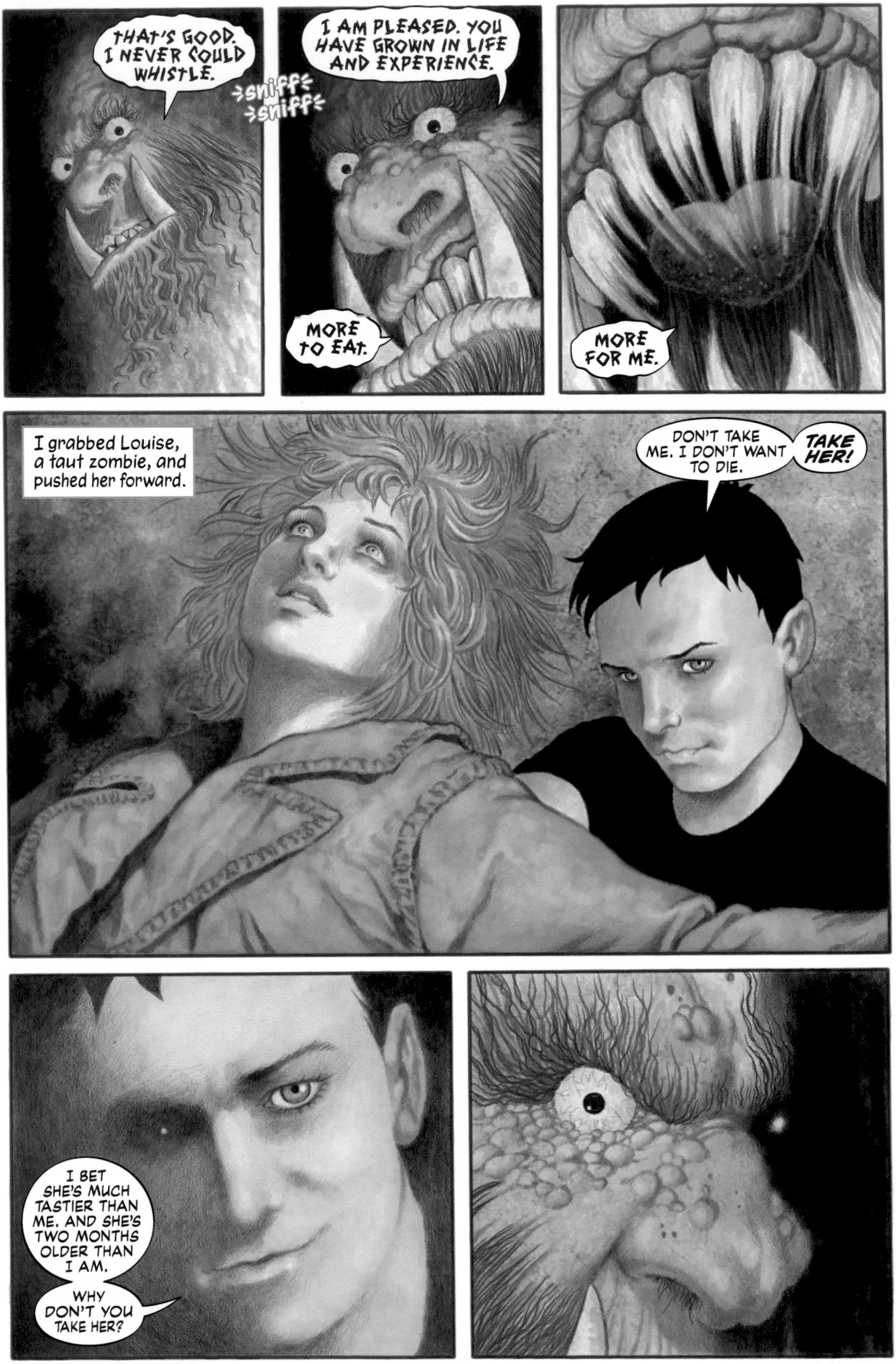

THAT'S GOOD. I NEVER COULD WHISTLE.
sniff sniff
I AM PLEASED. YOU HAVE GROWN IN LIFE AND EXPERIENCE.
MORE TO EAT.
MORE FOR ME.
I grabbed Louise, a taut zombie, and pushed her forward.
DON'T TAKE ME. I DON'T WANT TO DIE.
TAKE HER!
I BET SHE'S MUCH TASTIER THAN ME. AND SHE'S TWO MONTHS OLDER THAN I AM.
WHY DON'T YOU TAKE HER?

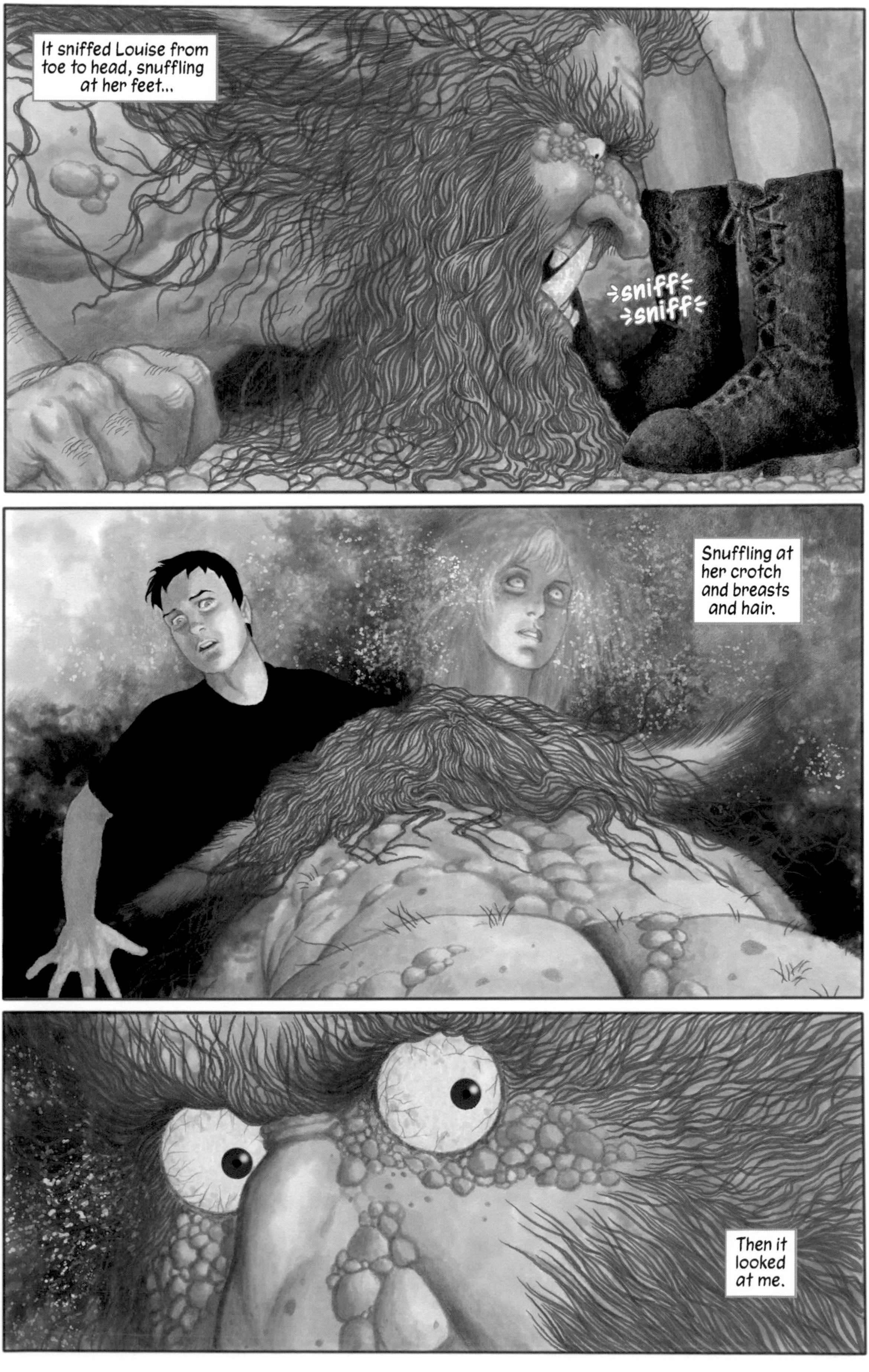
It sniffed Louise from toe to head, snuffling at her feet...
sniff sniff
Snuffling at her crotch and breasts and hair.
Then it looked at me.

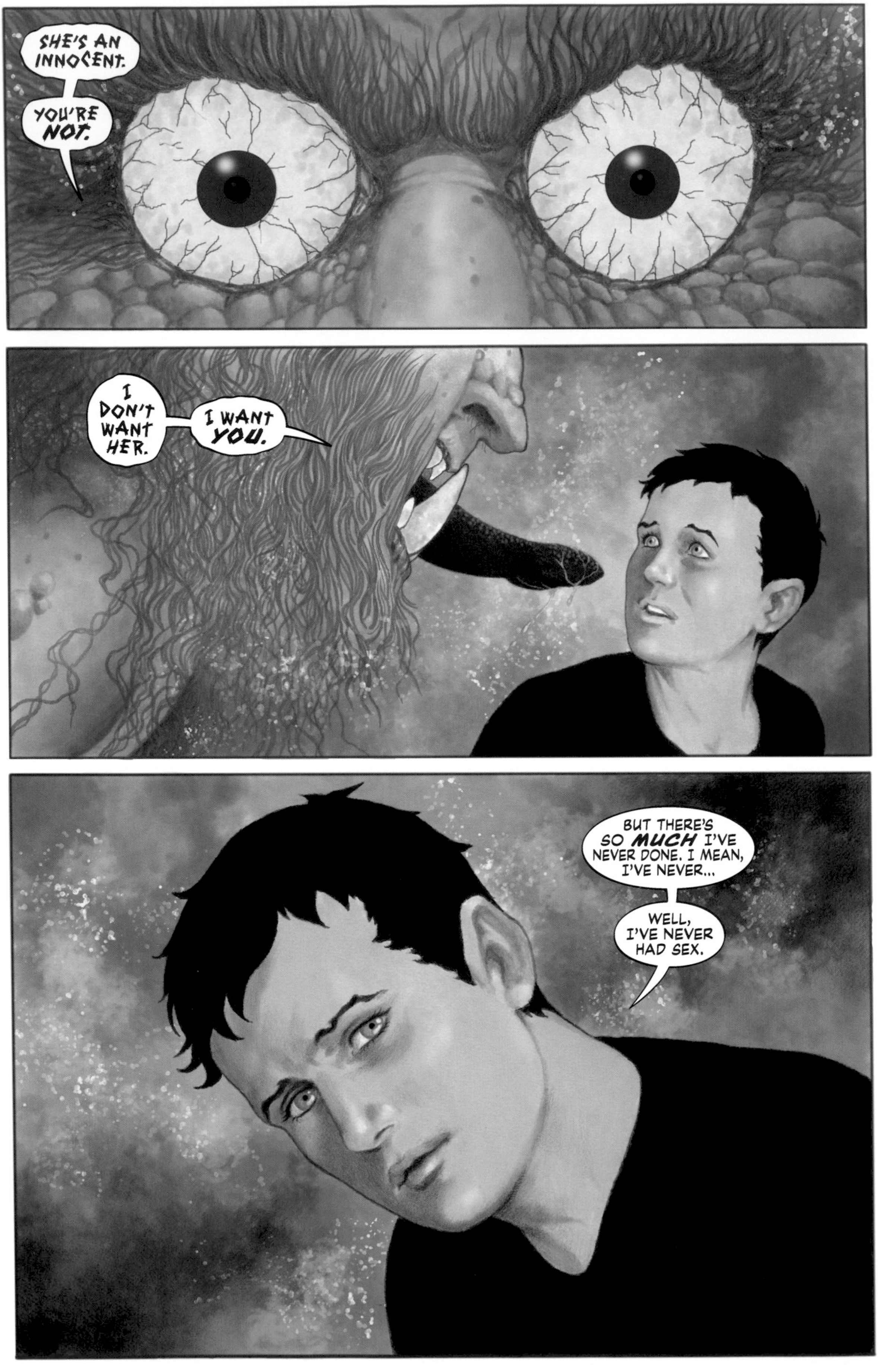

SHE'S AN INNOCENT.
YOU'RE NOT.
I DON'T WANT HER.
I WANT YOU.
BUT THERE'S SO MUCH I'VE NEVER DONE. I MEAN, I'VE NEVER...
WELL, I'VE NEVER HAD SEX.

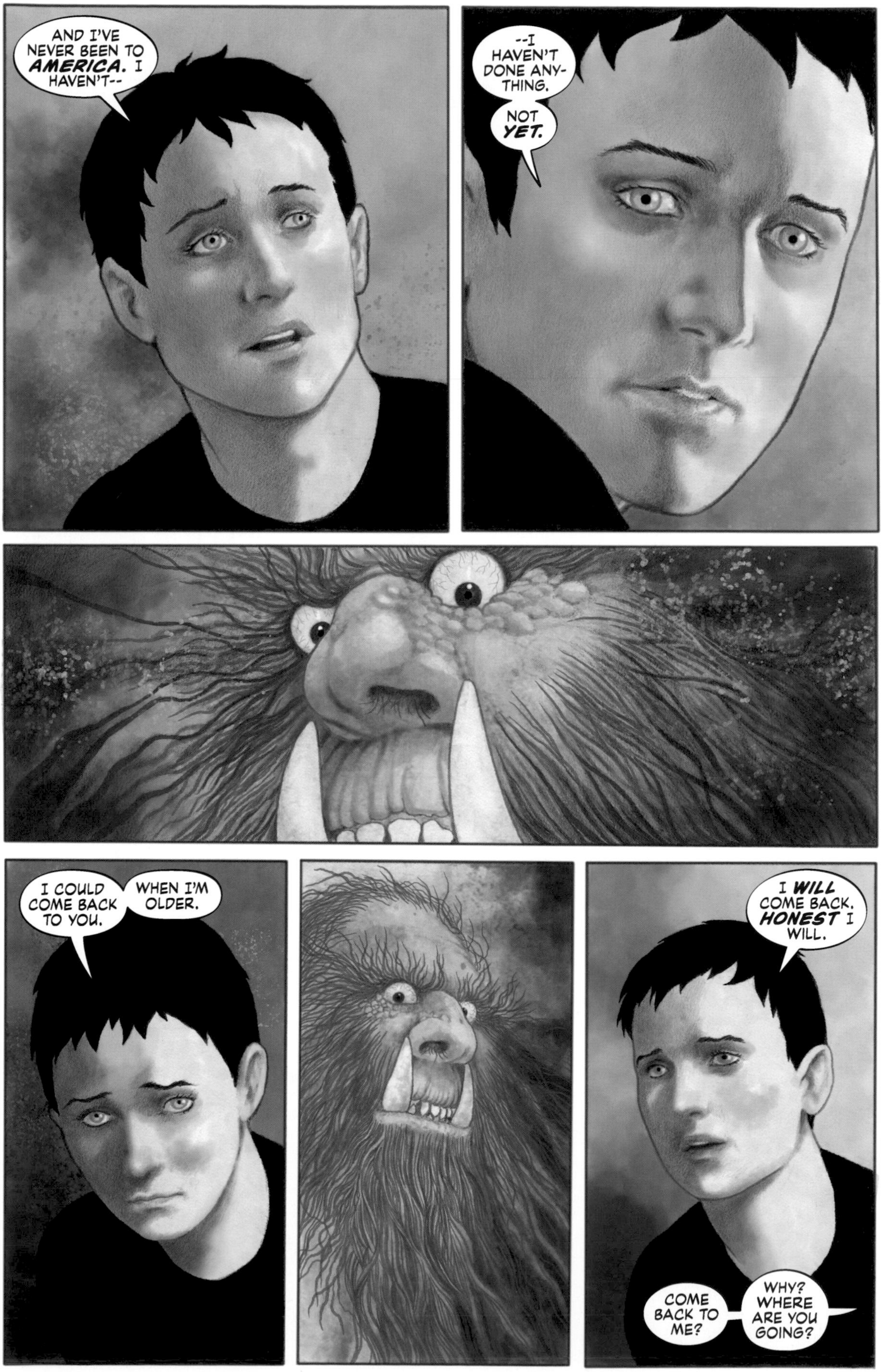
AND I'VE NEVER BEEN TO **AMERICA.** I HAVEN'T--
--I HAVEN'T DONE ANYTHING.
NOT **YET.**
I COULD COME BACK TO YOU.
WHEN I'M OLDER.
I **WILL** COME BACK. **HONEST** I WILL.
COME BACK TO ME?
WHY? WHERE ARE YOU GOING?

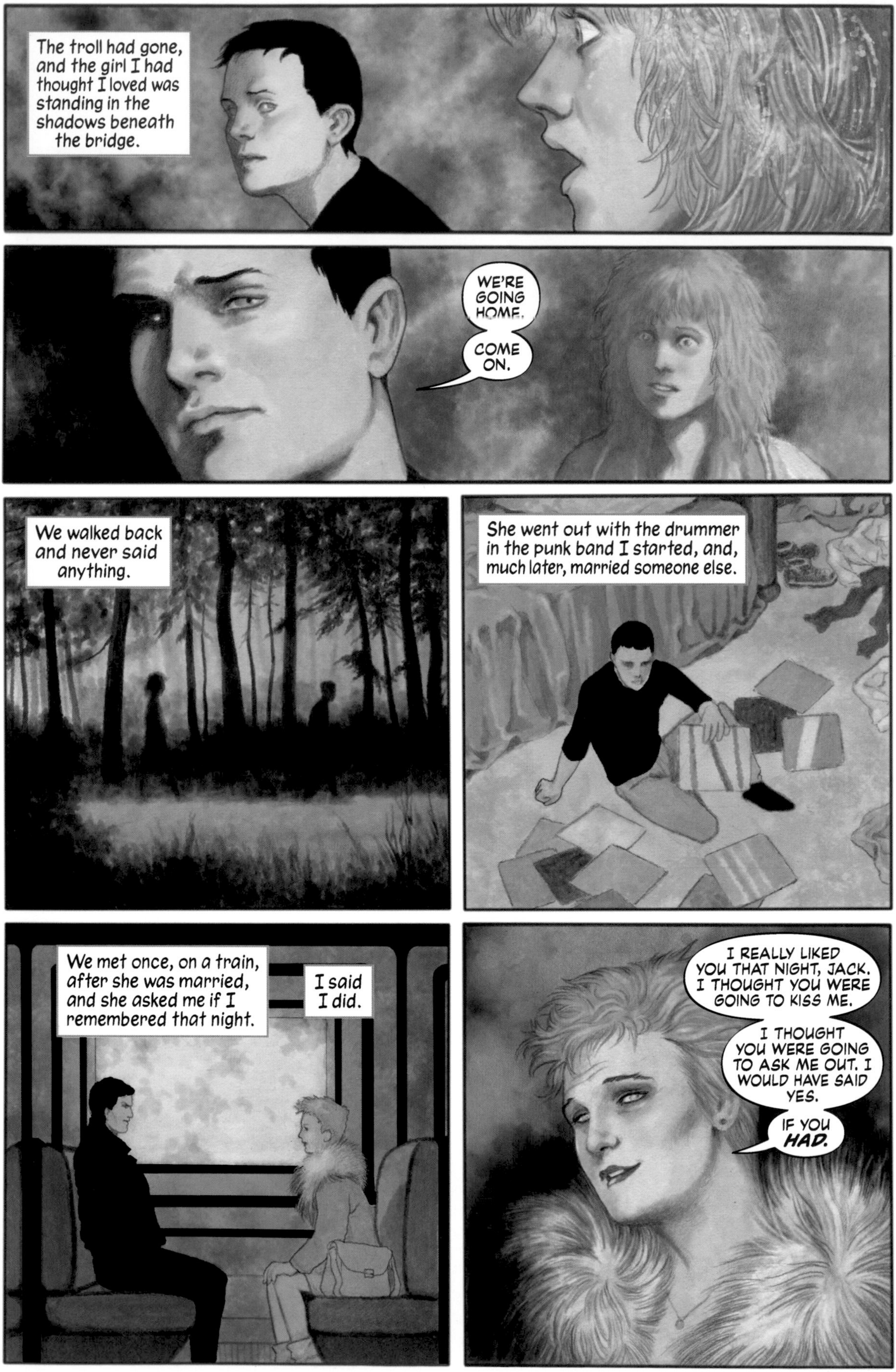
The troll had gone, and the girl I had thought I loved was standing in the shadows beneath the bridge.
WE'RE GOING HOME.
COME ON.
We walked back and never said anything.
She went out with the drummer in the punk band I started, and, much later, married someone else.
We met once, on a train, after she was married, and she asked me if I remembered that night.
I said I did.
I REALLY LIKED YOU THAT NIGHT, JACK. I THOUGHT YOU WERE GOING TO KISS ME.
I THOUGHT YOU WERE GOING TO ASK ME OUT. I WOULD HAVE SAID YES.
IF YOU HAD.

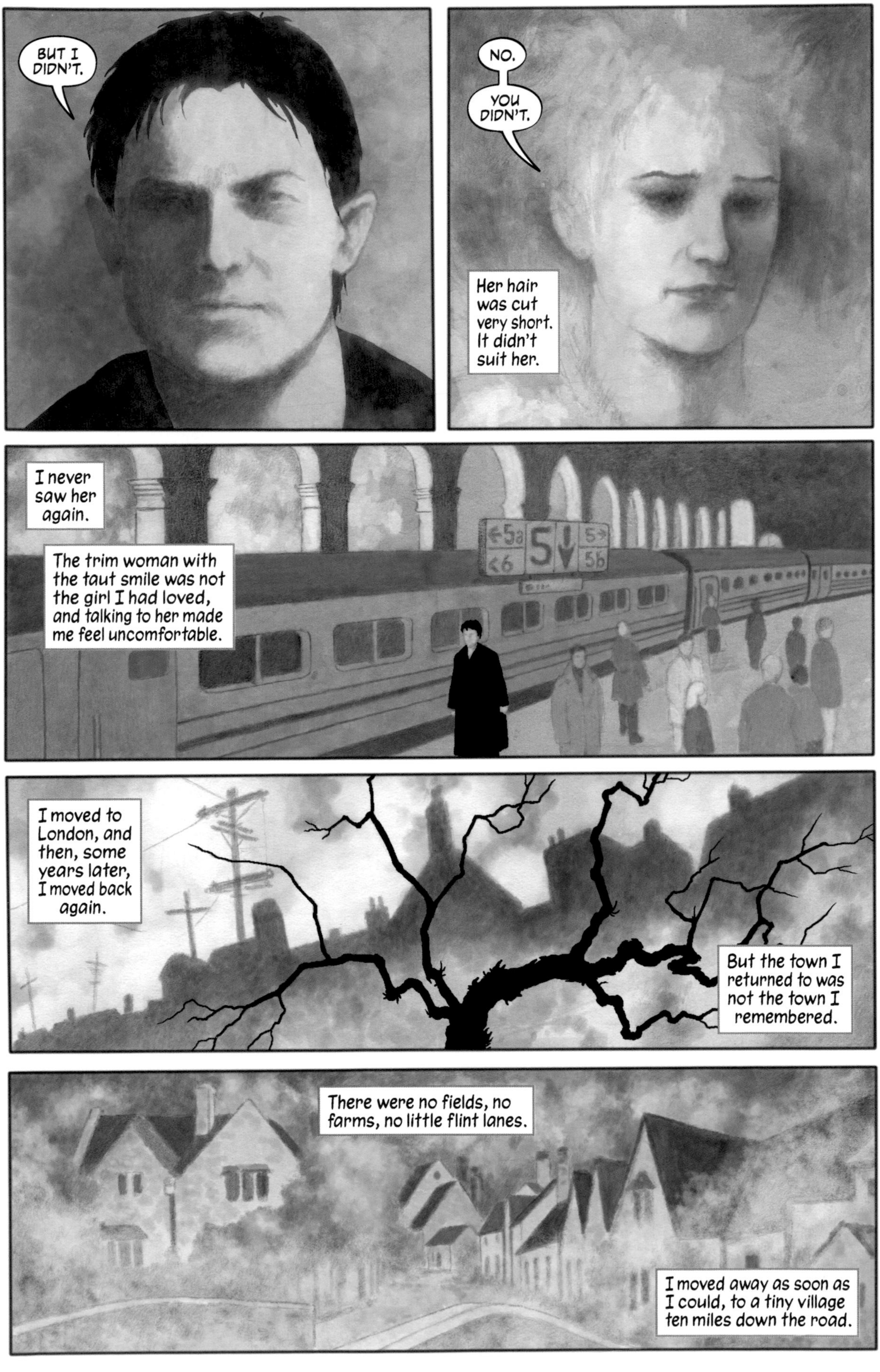
BUT I DIDN'T.
NO.
YOU DIDN'T.
Her hair was cut very short. It didn't suit her.
I never saw her again.
←5a 5 5→
←6 5b
The trim woman with the taut smile was not the girl I had loved, and talking to her made me feel uncomfortable.
I moved to London, and then, some years later, I moved back again.
But the town I returned to was not the town I remembered.
There were no fields, no farms, no little flint lanes.
I moved away as soon as I could, to a tiny village ten miles down the road.

I moved with my family-- I was married by now, with a toddler--

--into an old house that had once, many years before, been a railway station.

The tracks had been dug up, and the old couple who lived opposite us used it to grow vegetables.

I was getting older.

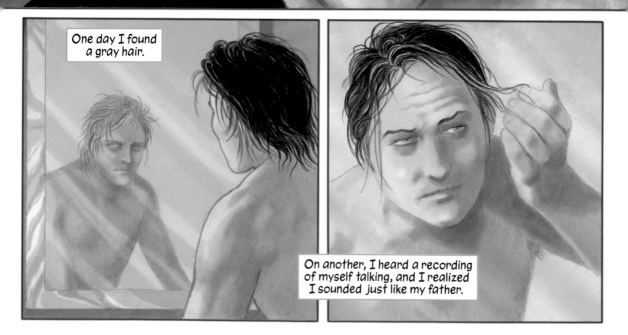

One day I found a gray hair.

On another, I heard a recording of myself talking, and I realized I sounded just like my father.

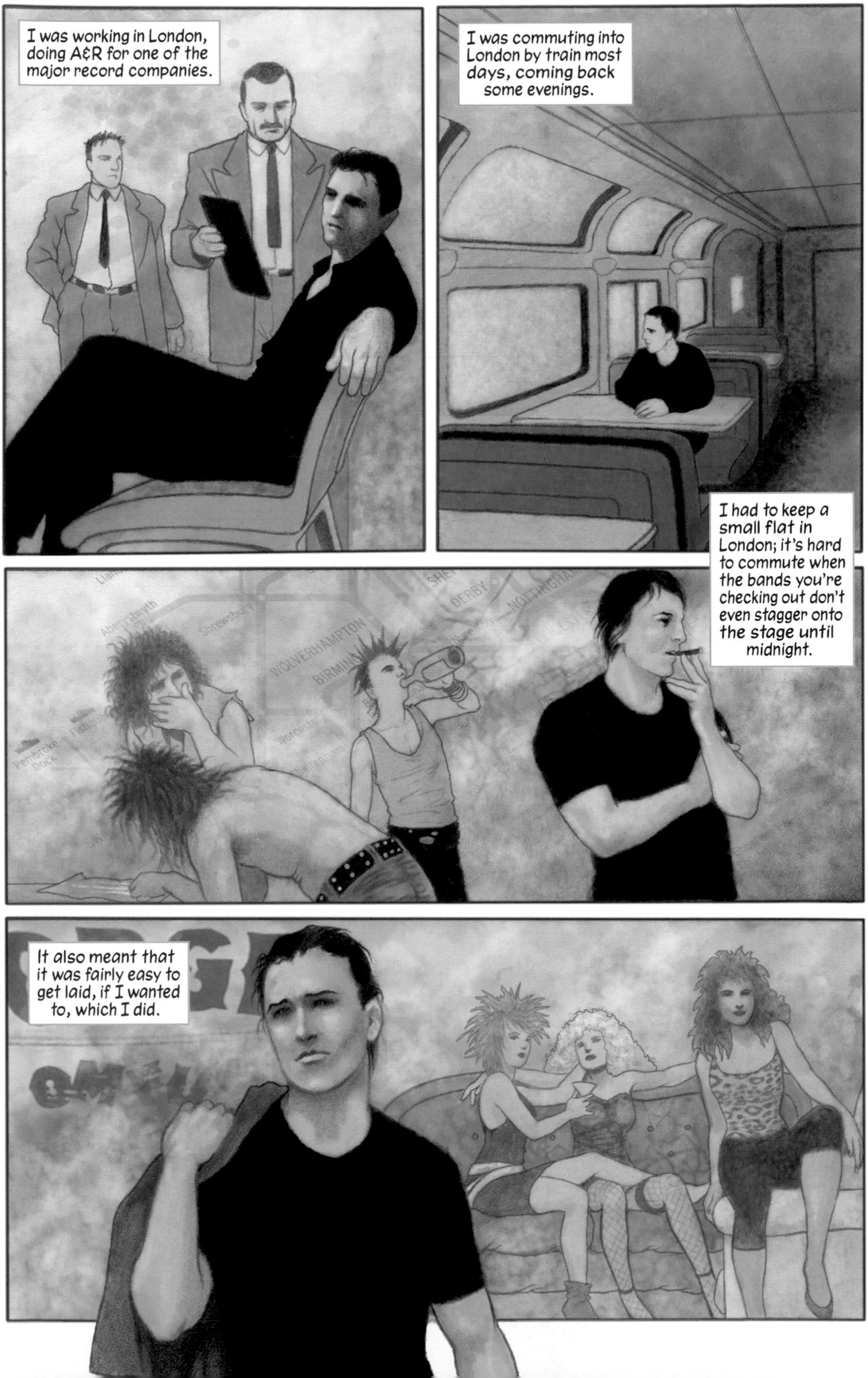

I was working in London, doing A&R for one of the major record companies.
I was commuting into London by train most days, coming back some evenings.
I had to keep a small flat in London; it's hard to commute when the bands you're checking out don't even stagger onto the stage until midnight.
Aberystwyth
Shrewsbury
WOLVERHAMPTON
DERBY
Pembroke Dock
It also meant that it was fairly easy to get laid, if I wanted to, which I did.

I thought that Eleanora--that was my wife's name; I should have mentioned that before, I suppose--didn't know about the other women.
But I got back from a two-week jaunt to New York one winter's day, and when I arrived at the house it was empty and cold.
She had left a letter, not a note.
really dont love me
and you never did

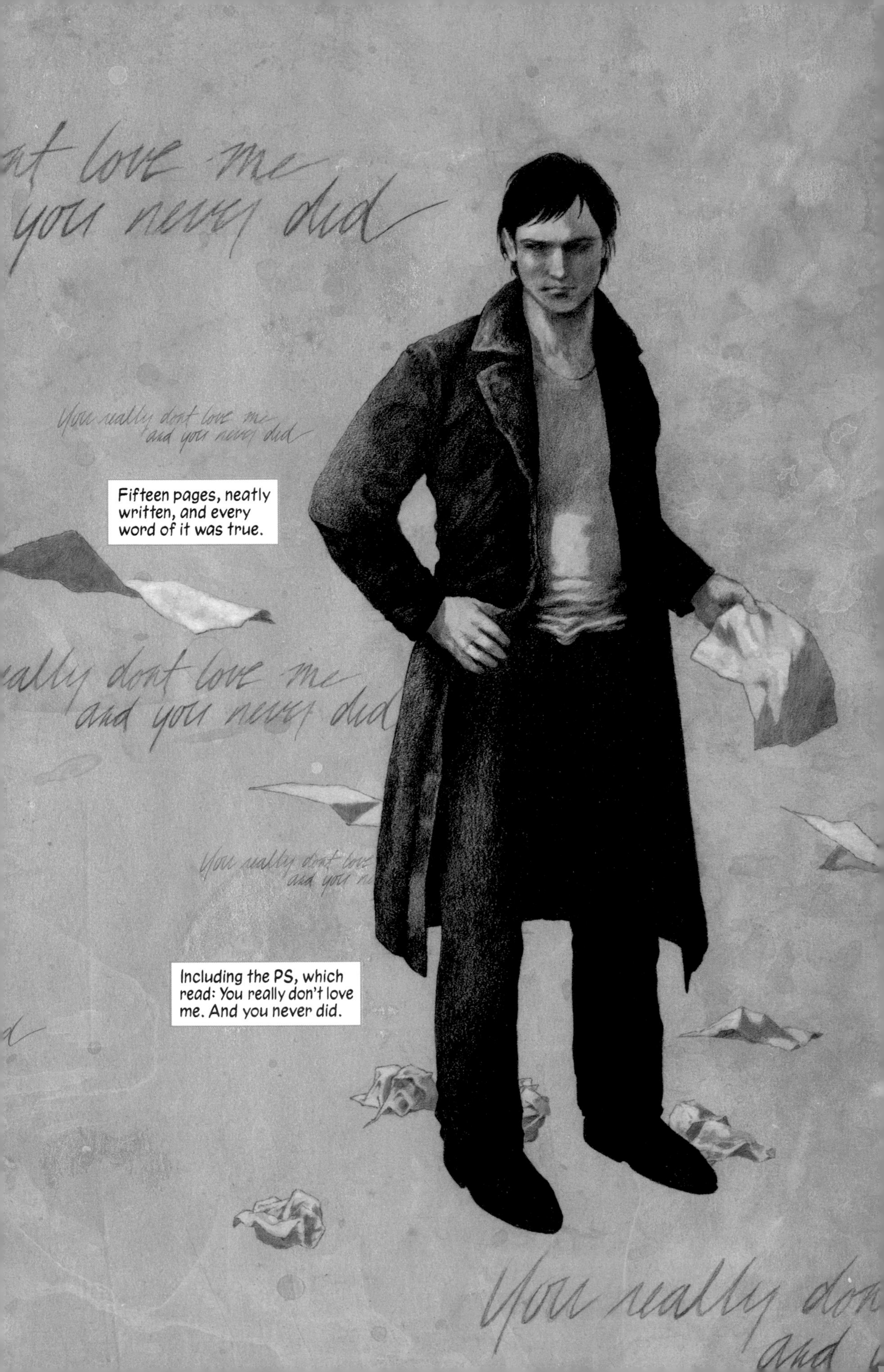
You really dont love me
and you never did
Fifteen pages, neatly written, and every word of it was true.
Including the PS, which read: You really don't love me. And you never did.

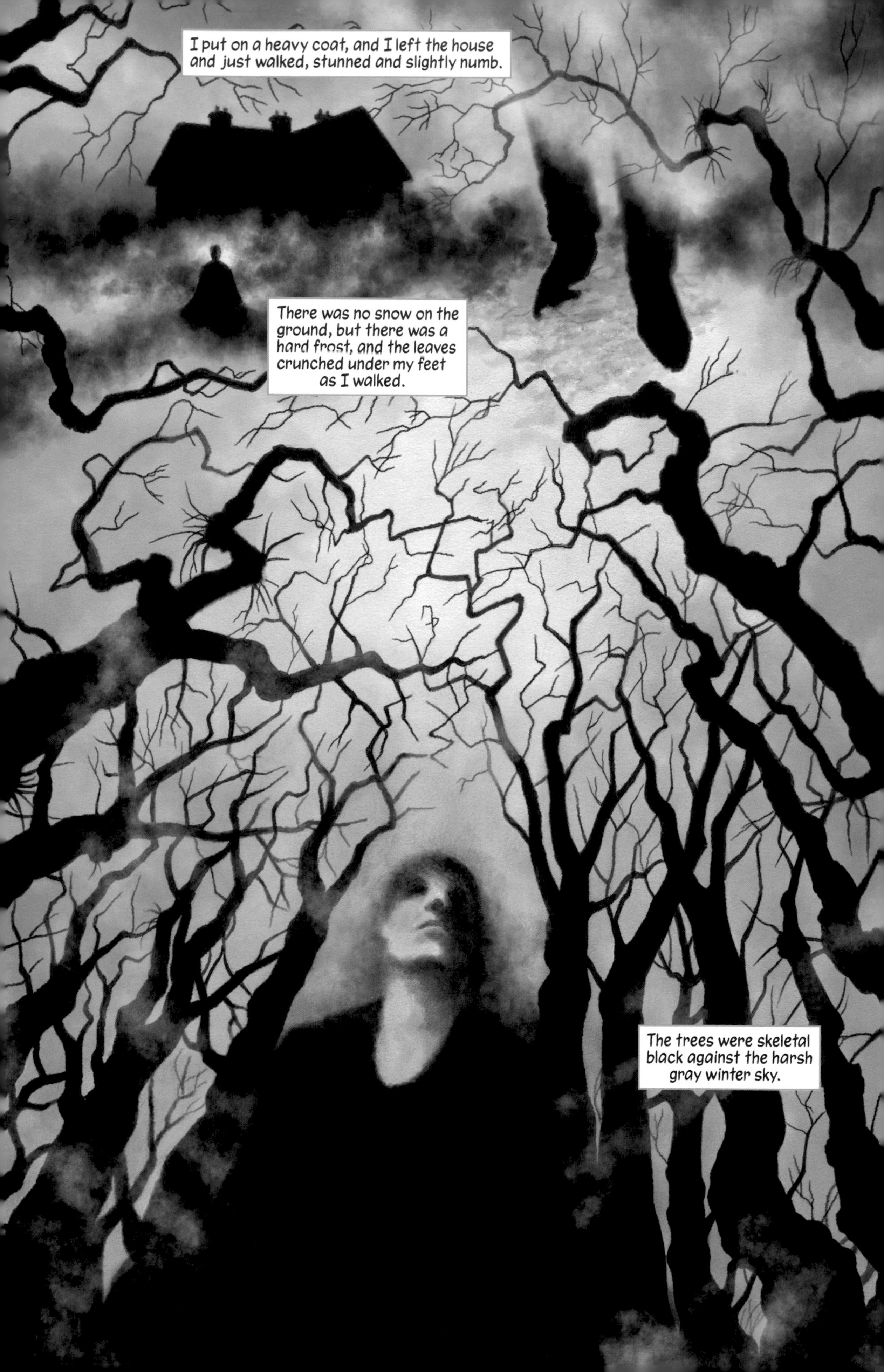
I put on a heavy coat, and I left the house and just walked, stunned and slightly numb.
There was no snow on the ground, but there was a hard frost, and the leaves crunched under my feet as I walked.
The trees were skeletal black against the harsh gray winter sky.

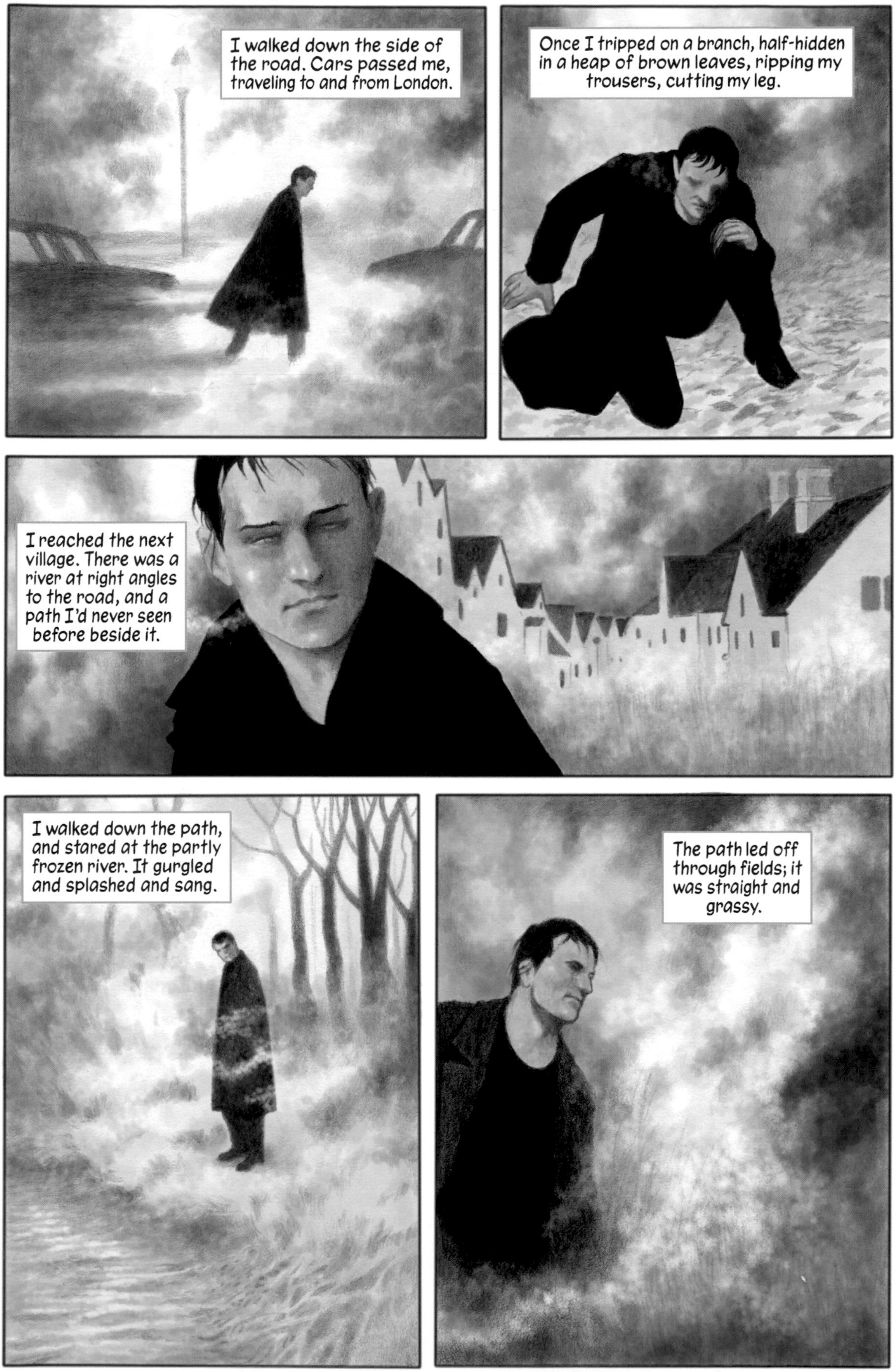
I walked down the side of the road. Cars passed me, traveling to and from London.
Once I tripped on a branch, half-hidden in a heap of brown leaves, ripping my trousers, cutting my leg.
I reached the next village. There was a river at right angles to the road, and a path I'd never seen before beside it.
I walked down the path, and stared at the partly frozen river. It gurgled and splashed and sang.
The path led off through fields; it was straight and grassy.

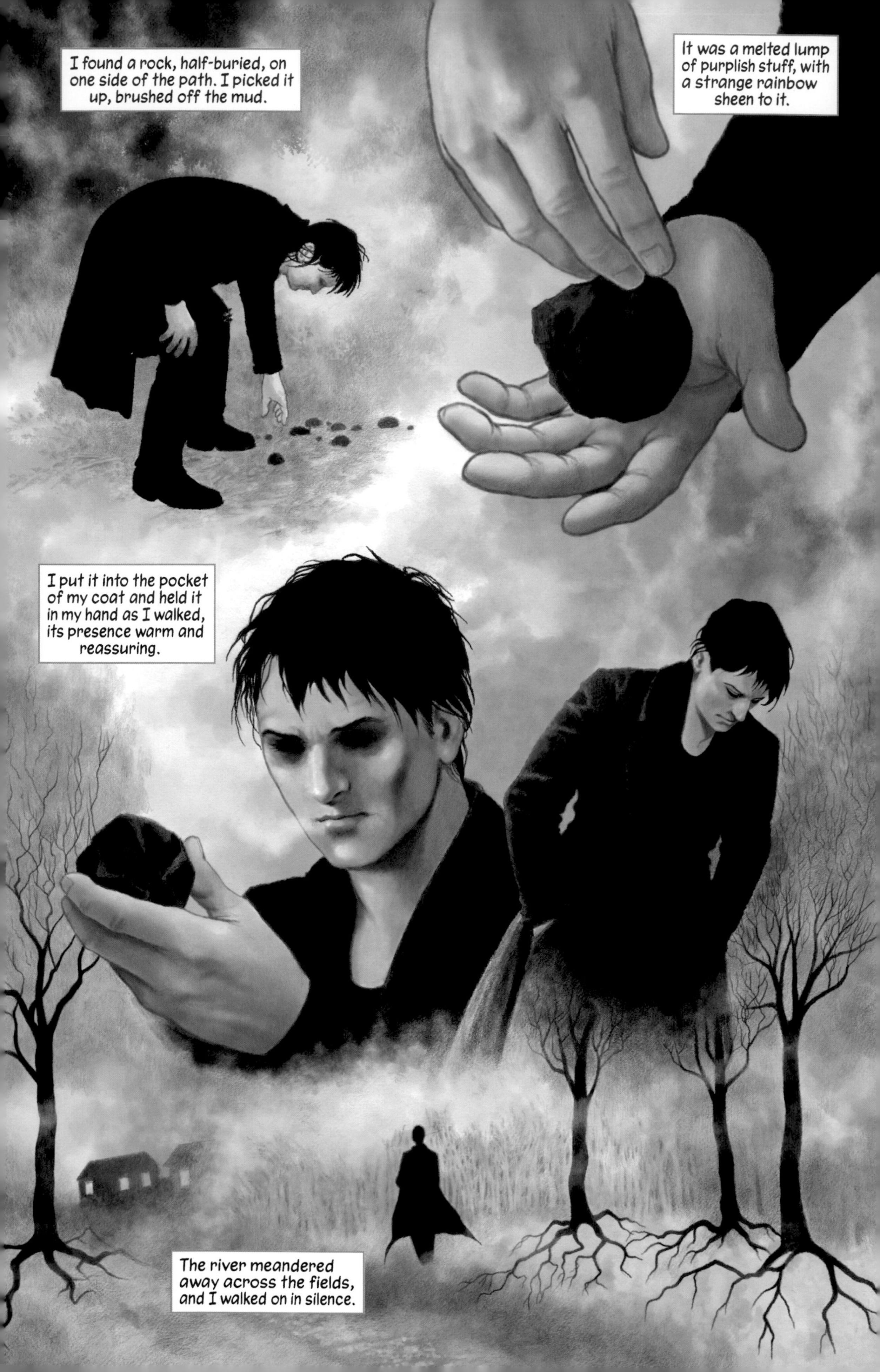
I found a rock, half-buried, on one side of the path. I picked it up, brushed off the mud.
It was a melted lump of purplish stuff, with a strange rainbow sheen to it.
I put it into the pocket of my coat and held it in my hand as I walked, its presence warm and reassuring.
The river meandered away across the fields, and I walked on in silence.

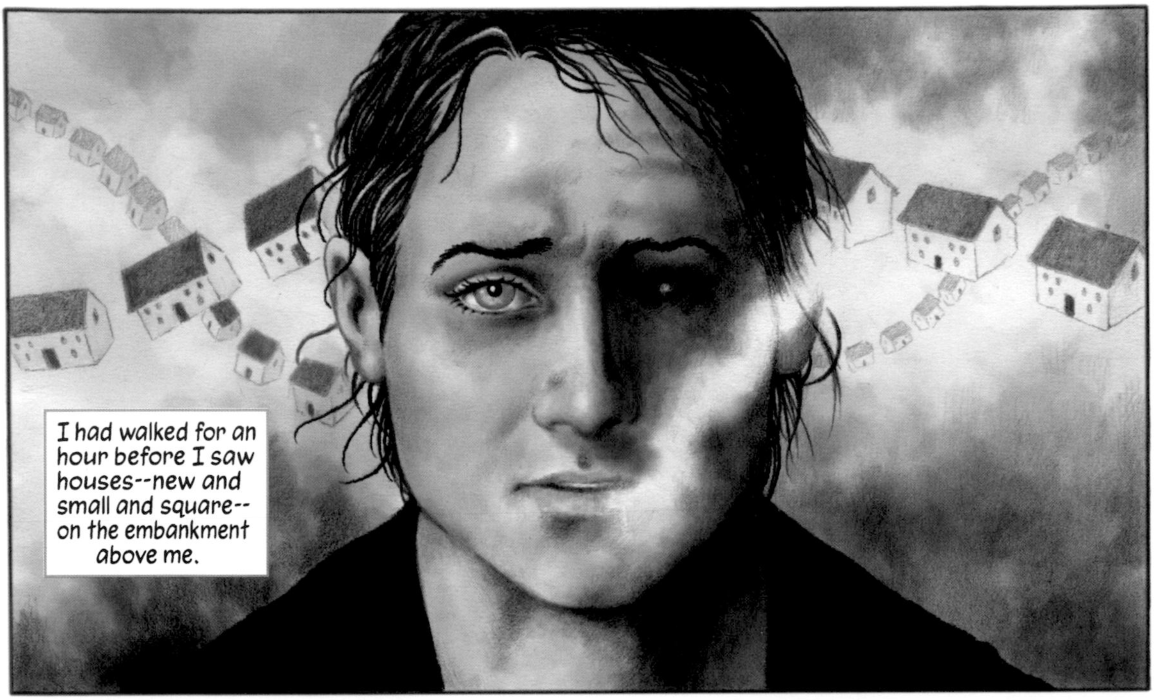
I had walked for an hour before I saw houses--new and small and square--on the embankment above me.

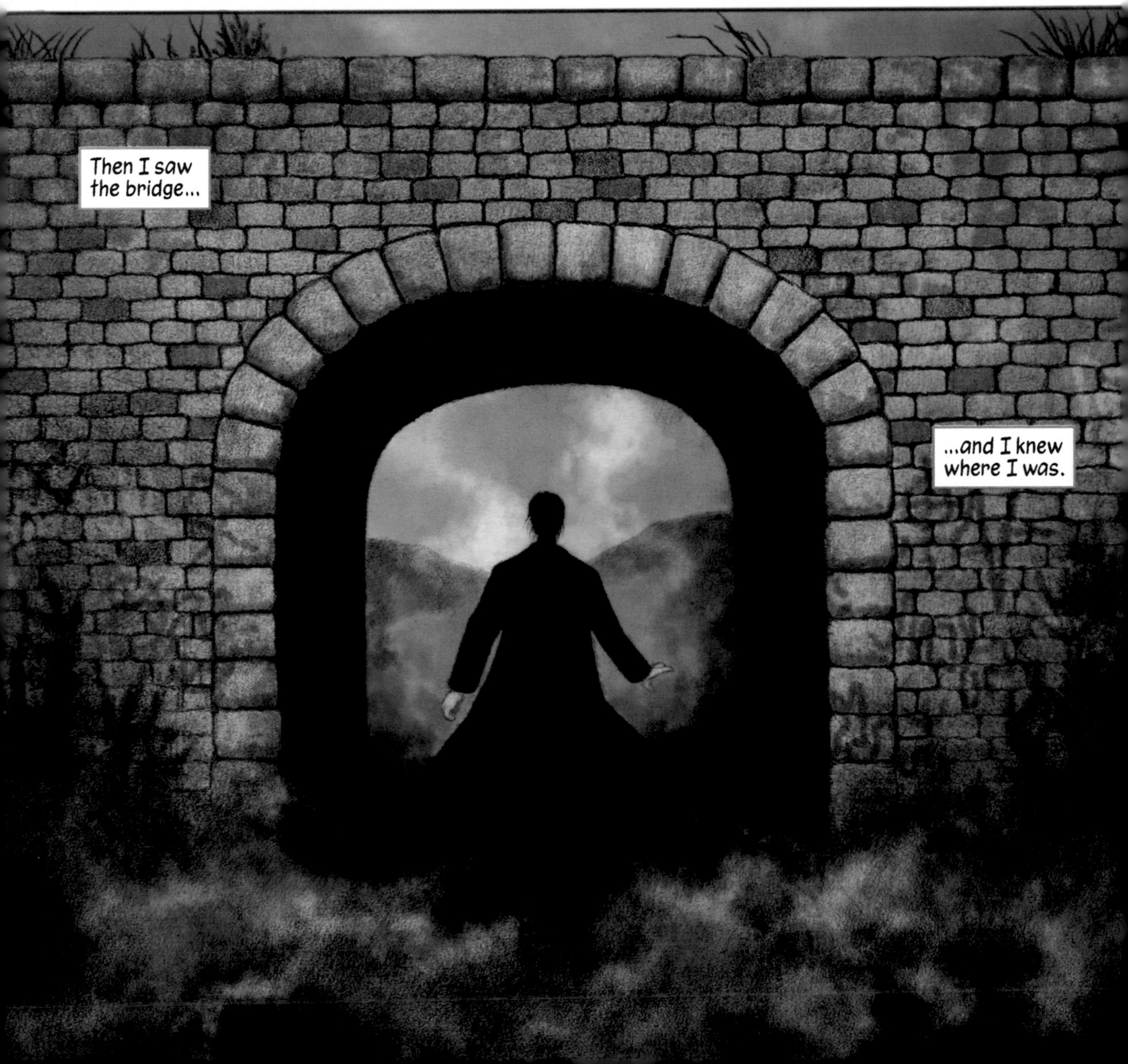
Then I saw the bridge...
...and I knew where I was.

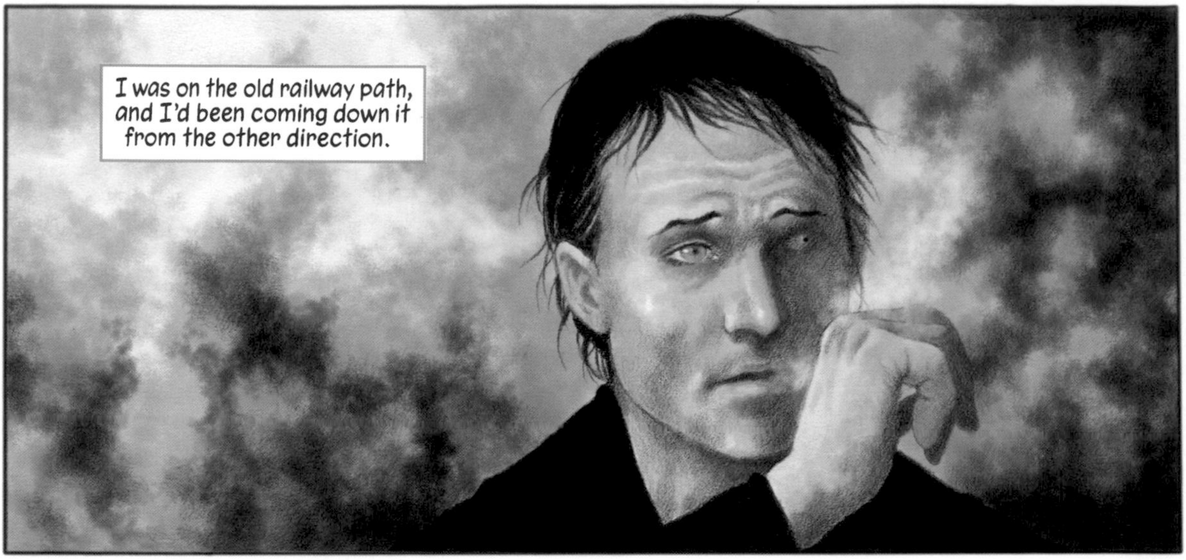
I was on the old railway path, and I'd been coming down it from the other direction.

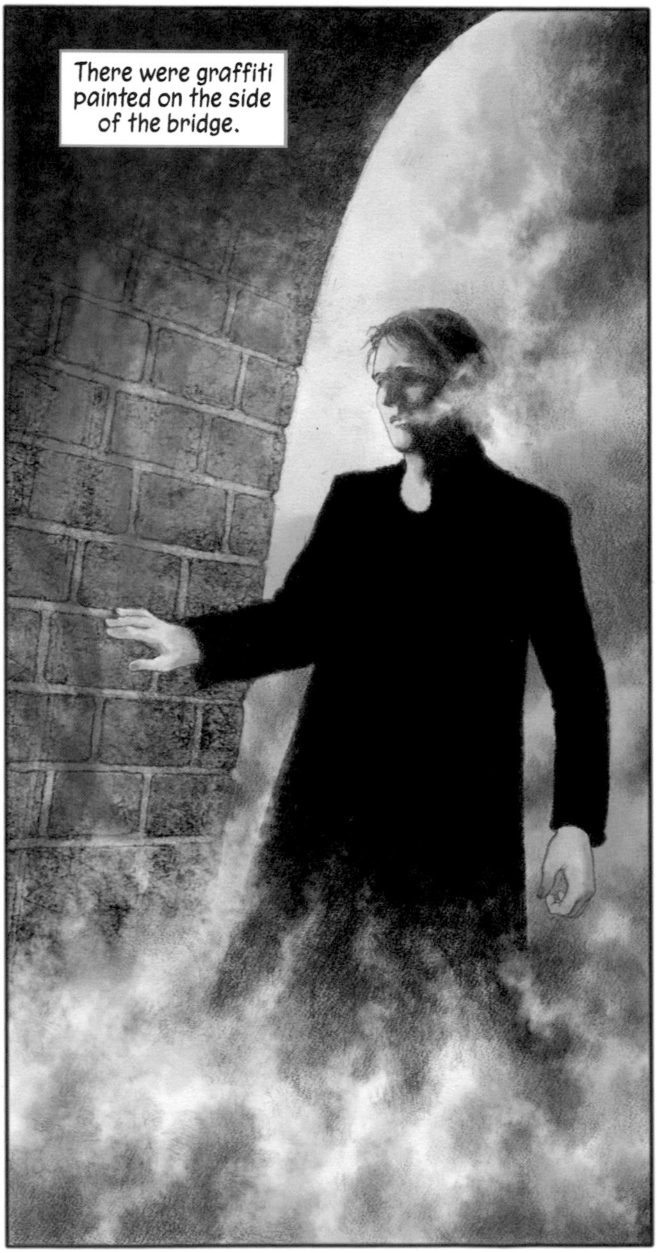
There were graffiti painted on the side of the bridge.

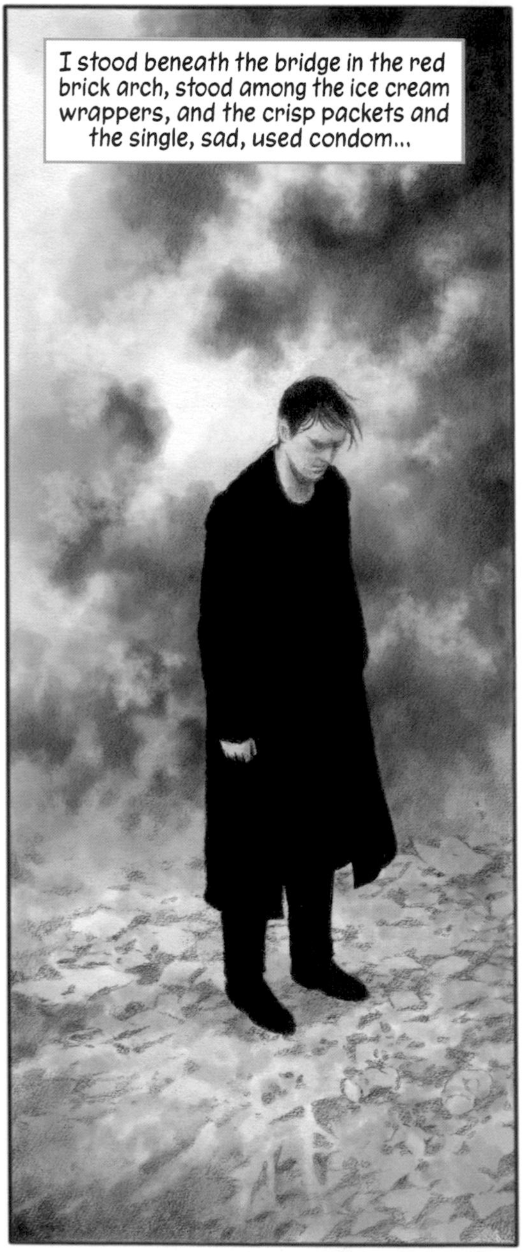
I stood beneath the bridge in the red brick arch, stood among the ice cream wrappers, and the crisp packets and the single, sad, used condom...

I watched my breath steam in the cold afternoon air.

The blood had dried into my trousers.

Cars passed over the bridge above me; I could hear a radio playing loudly in one of them.

HELLO?

I said quietly, feeling embarrassed, feeling foolish.

HELLO?

There was no answer. The wind rustled the crisp packets and the leaves.

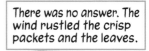

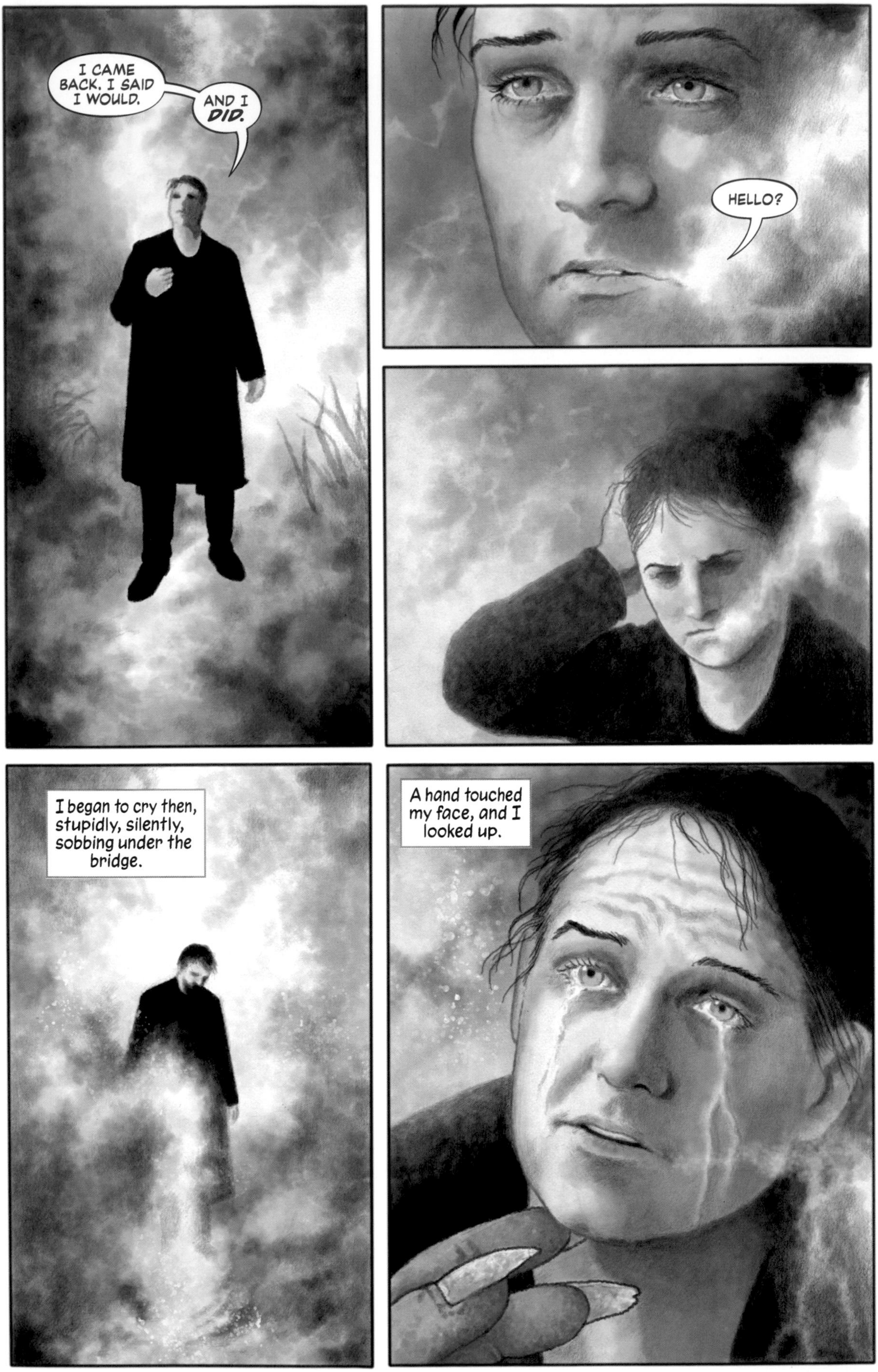
I CAME BACK. I SAID I WOULD.
AND I *DID.*
HELLO?
I began to cry then, stupidly, silently, sobbing under the bridge.
A hand touched my face, and I looked up.

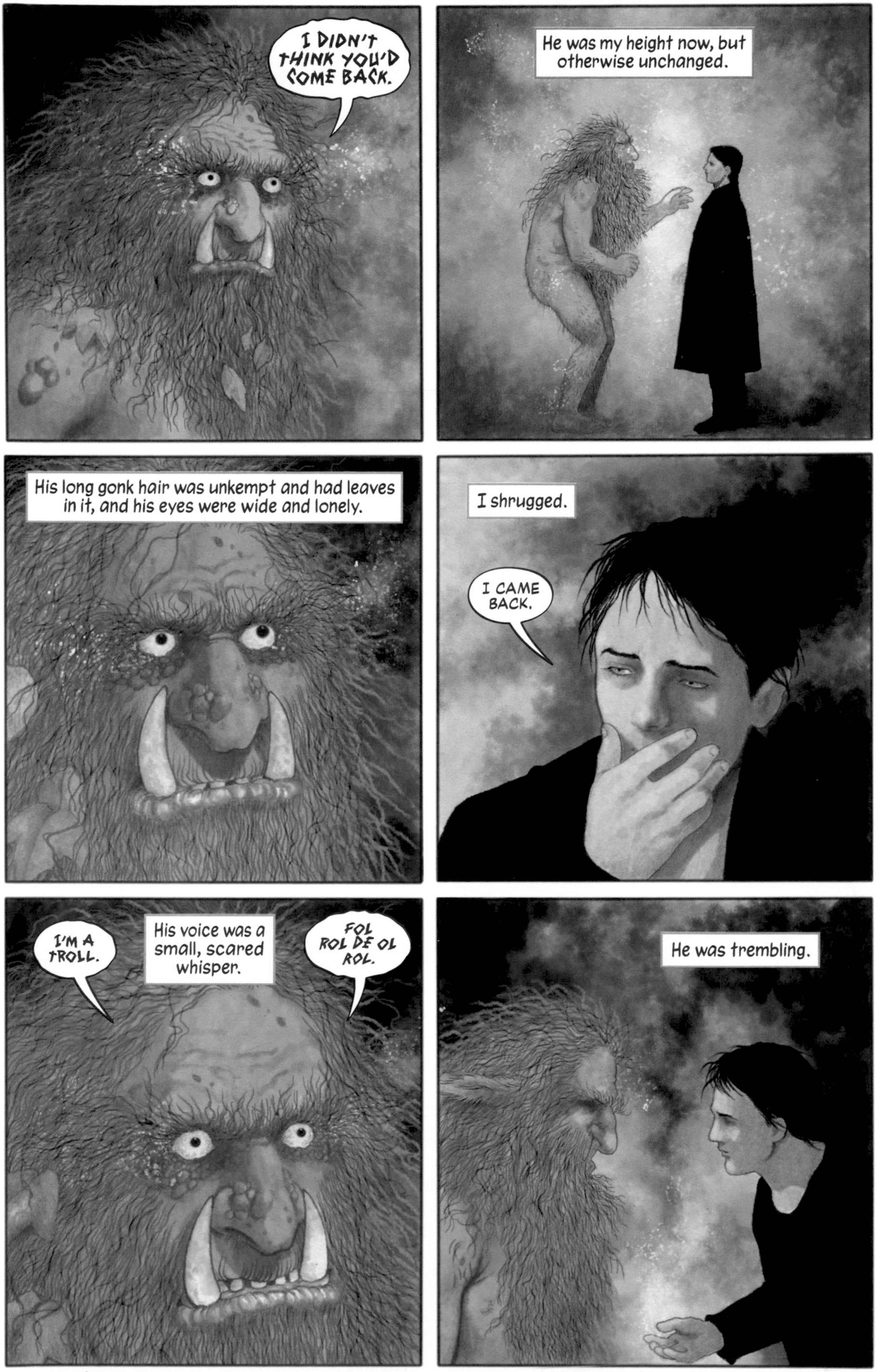

I DIDN'T THINK YOU'D COME BACK.
He was my height now, but otherwise unchanged.
His long gonk hair was unkempt and had leaves in it, and his eyes were wide and lonely.
I shrugged.
I CAME BACK.
I'M A TROLL.
His voice was a small, scared whisper.
FOL ROL DE OL ROL.
He was trembling.

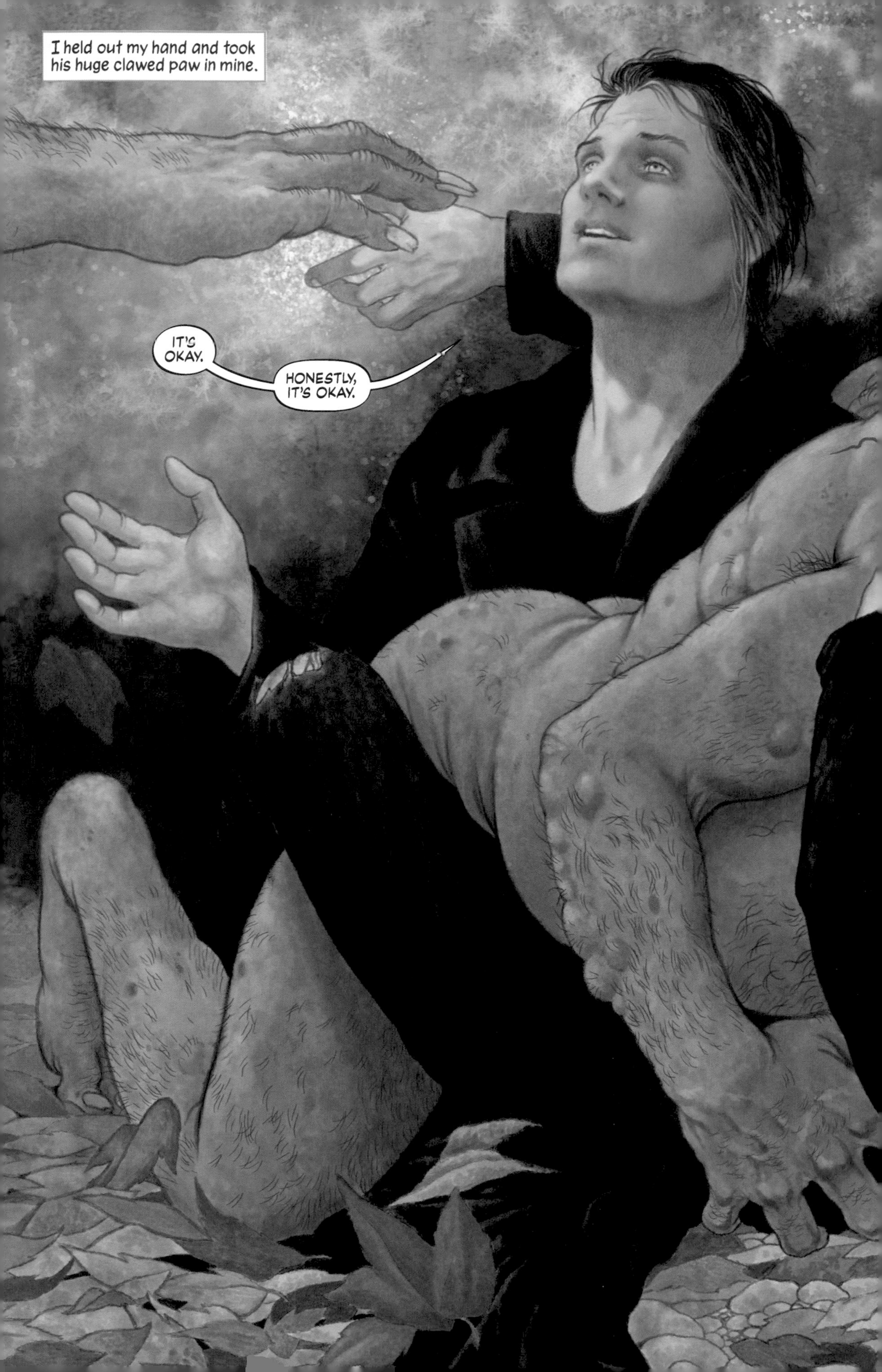
I held out my hand and took his huge clawed paw in mine.
IT'S OKAY.
HONESTLY, IT'S OKAY.

He pushed me to the ground, onto the leaves and the wrappers and the condom...
...and lowered himself on top of me.
Then he raised his head, and opened his mouth...
...and ate my life with his strong sharp teeth.

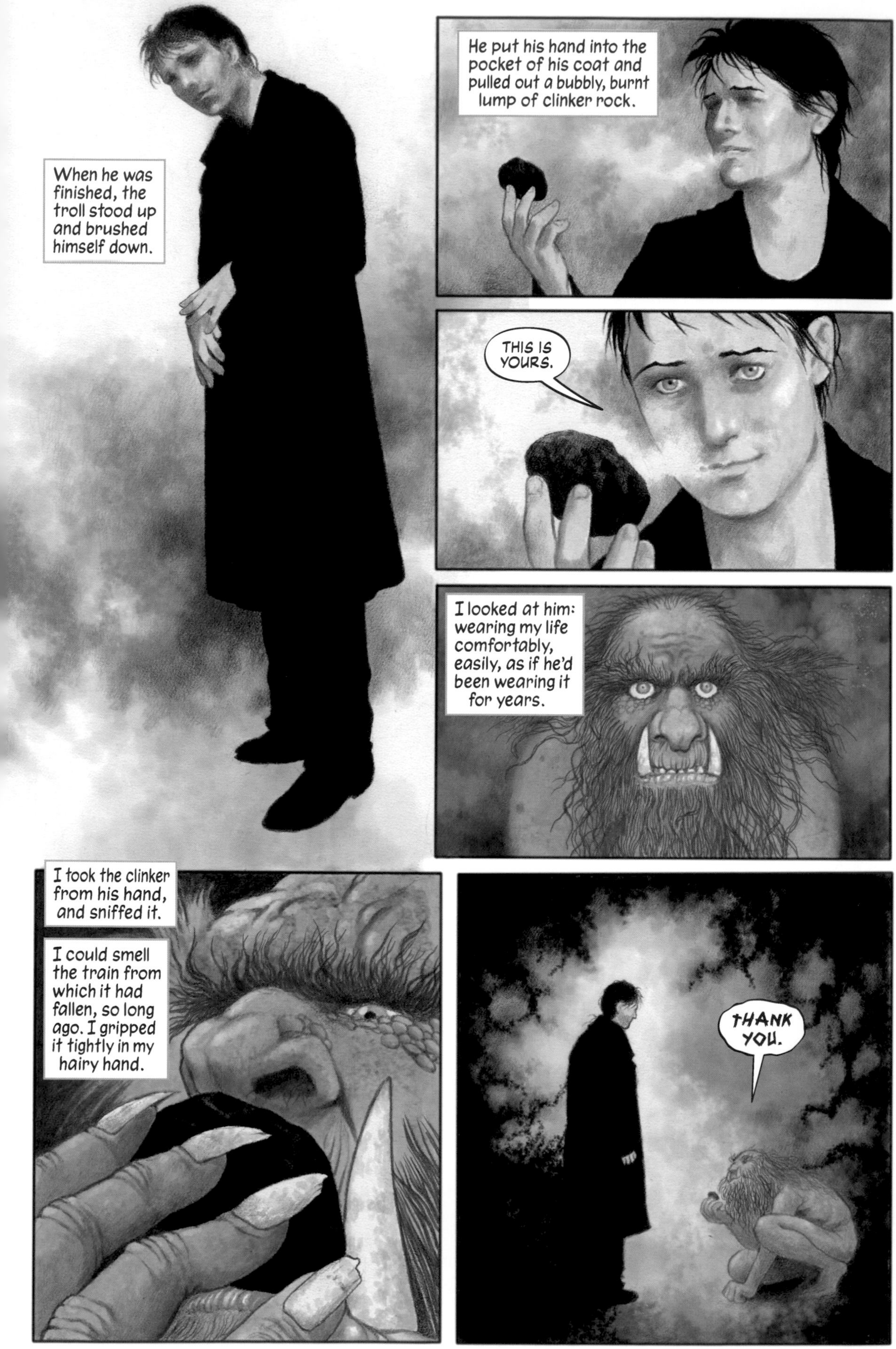
When he was finished, the troll stood up and brushed himself down.
He put his hand into the pocket of his coat and pulled out a bubbly, burnt lump of clinker rock.
THIS IS YOURS.
I looked at him: wearing my life comfortably, easily, as if he'd been wearing it for years.
I took the clinker from his hand, and sniffed it.
I could smell the train from which it had fallen, so long ago. I gripped it tightly in my hairy hand.
THANK YOU.

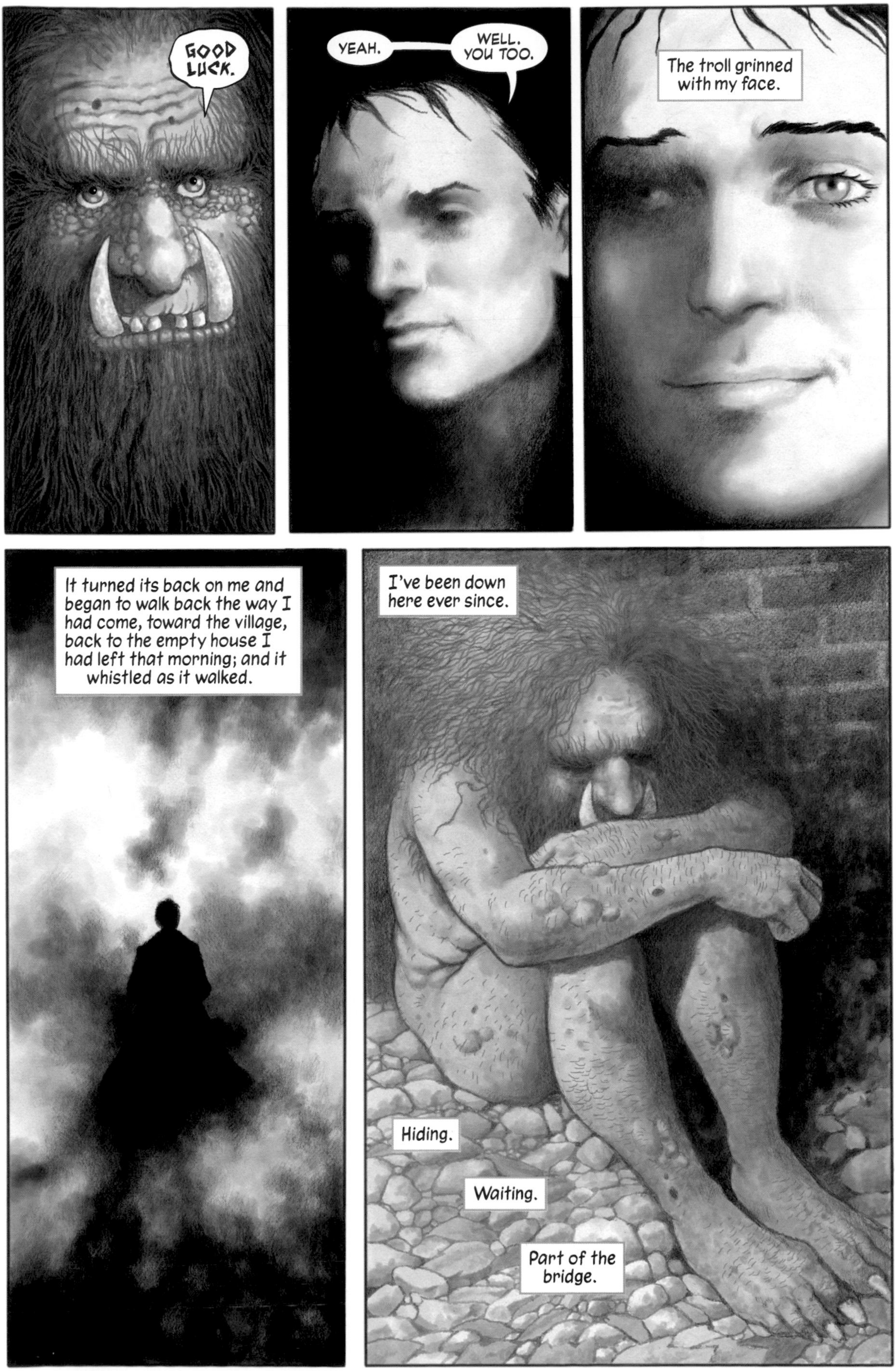
GOOD LUCK.
YEAH.
WELL. YOU TOO.
The troll grinned with my face.
It turned its back on me and began to walk back the way I had come, toward the village, back to the empty house I had left that morning; and it whistled as it walked.
I've been down here ever since.
Hiding.
Waiting.
Part of the bridge.

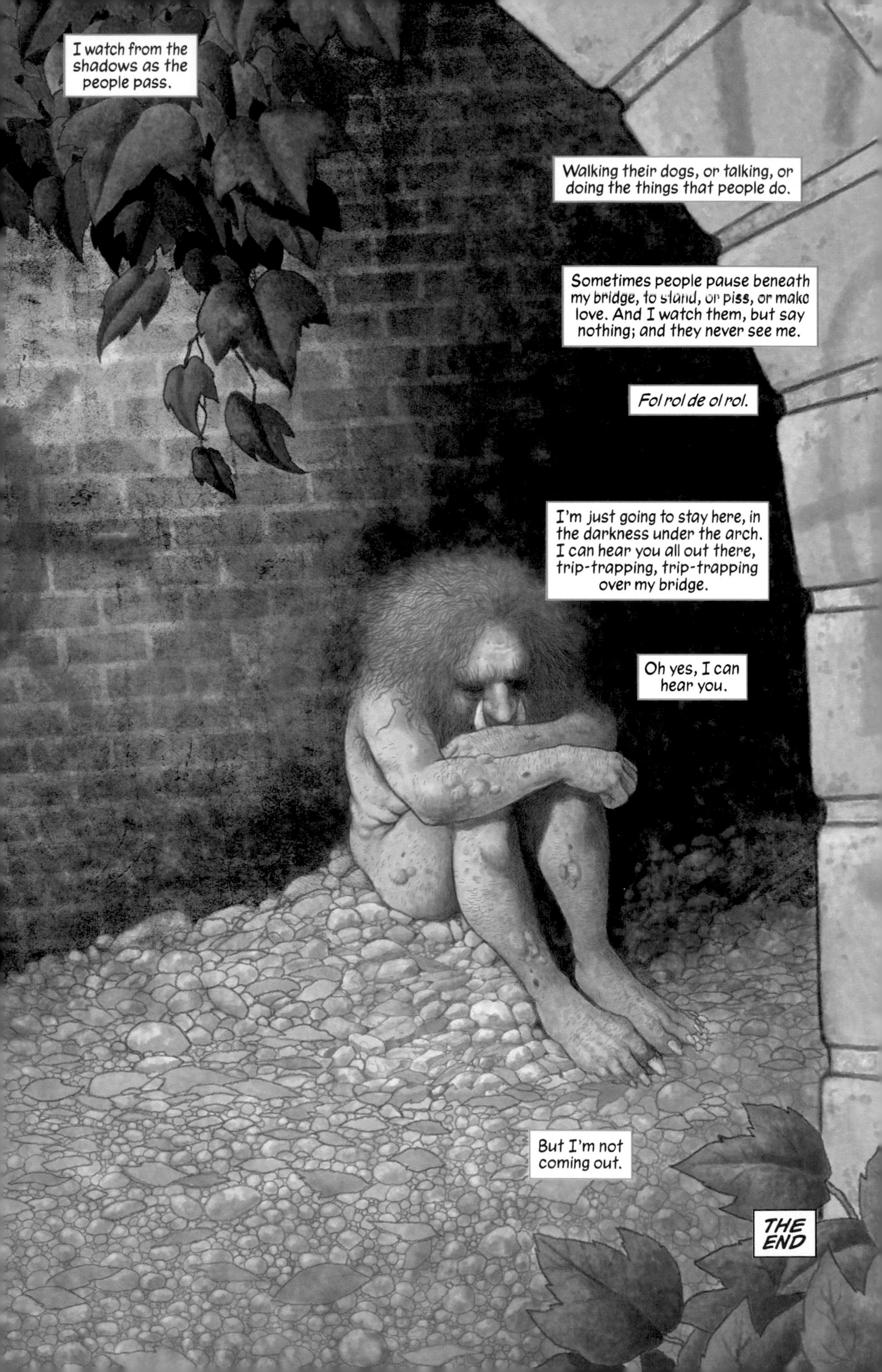
I watch from the shadows as the people pass.
Walking their dogs, or talking, or doing the things that people do.
Sometimes people pause beneath my bridge, to stand, or piss, or make love. And I watch them, but say nothing; and they never see me.
Fol rol de ol rol.
I'm just going to stay here, in the darkness under the arch. I can hear you all out there, trip-trapping, trip-trapping over my bridge.
Oh yes, I can hear you.
But I'm not coming out.
THE END

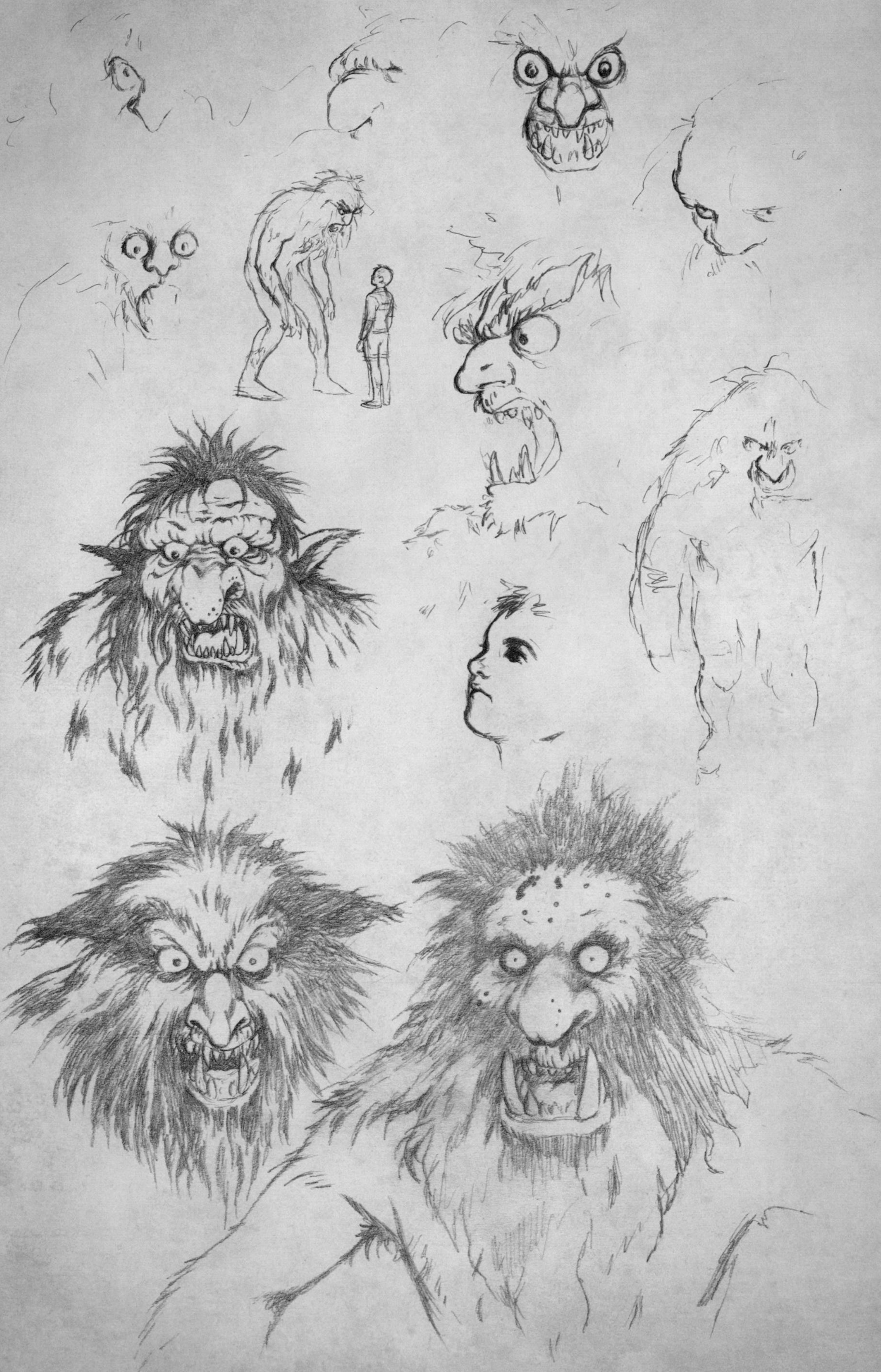